"Debbie Garvey has produced an engaging and thought-provoking book that examines and demystifies a wealth of knowledge from research, helping early years practitioners to think carefully and critically about their work with young children. The book is remarkable, both for the clarity with which it explains complex theories and concepts, and the deftness with which the relevance of those theories and concepts to everyday practice is explored. Insights from neuroscience and early brain development are placed in a broader context, making links to ideas from early years pioneers, and to other academic fields such as anthropology. The case studies that pop up throughout the book [...] serve to place these ideas directly into a range of practice contexts, drawing on and celebrating the work of practitioners [...]. The book is presented as a journey through these ideas, and the reader is encouraged to journey actively alongside the author, stopping regularly to review the road travelled and to reflect meaningfully on lessons learned and insights gained."
    – **Dr Yinka Olusoga**, *Lecturer in Education, University of Sheffield*

"What a treasure trove of learning! Not only does this book provide clean and clear reading material on the complexity of neuroscience, behaviour, psychology and the role of the adult; each chapter is filled with practical examples, and moments of pause and reflection throughout. [...] I was drawn in from the opening preface with the style of writing that simply and powerfully speaks to you. Generatively Debbie provides a wealth of signposting too, to other rich and informative resources that together with *Little Brains Matter* will aid any student, practitioner, lecturer or person(s) exploring the importance of little brains and why they matter."
    – **Dr Julie A. Ovington** AiMH, *Senior Lecturer and Program Leader in Childhood and Society Studies, University of Sunderland*

"This book is essential for anyone working in early years. Debbie's passion for the early childhood sector shines, and her research-informed experience comes across clearly on every page. Neuroscience is a complex field to get to grips with, but Debbie makes each key area accessible, explaining the incredible nature of the human brain and outlining what is needed for healthy neurological development. The case studies are truly thought provoking and offer practical takeaways […]. Above all, Debbie succeeds in her aim to empower educators, and throughout the book runs the golden thread of valuing children, tuning into them, and learning from them. A fantastic read."
– **Sarah Watkins**, *Author, Presenter and Lecturer, University of Worcester*

"In *Little Brains Matter* Debbie's generosity of spirit knows no bounds and her desire to share both her knowledge and her passion is palpable, not just through the accessibility of the jargon-free conversational style […] but in the immanently do-able ways in which sources are embedded into the very heart and soul of the text and not just listed dryly at chapter ends. `If you want to explore this more[…]', Debbie incites, `go to […]. I would urge you to explore it further' […] This is as much a book about how to explore and read around a subject matter as it is about the imparting of understanding. Although the latter it does aplenty."
– **Joanna Ainsworth**, *Early Years Montessori Researcher and Practitioner*

"As a foster carer we deal with all of these behaviours on a daily basis, but we often don't have any knowledge of the science behind it. It was amazing to read some of what I already know to be but didn't have a name for. Anyone working in child development would greatly benefit from reading this book, which raises as many questions as it answers on a never-ending but fascinating topic."

– **C. E. A. Forster**, *Foster Carer and Author of* You're Being Ridiculous

This accessible guide introduces neuroscience, demystifying terminology and language and increasing the knowledge, skills and, importantly, confidence of anyone interested in brain development in early childhood.

Practical and reflective chapters highlight the multi-faceted role of adults as 'brain builders' and encourage the reader to consider how the environment, play and interactions are crucially interlinked. The book considers cutting-edge science and introduces this in an accessible way to look at a range of ways that adults can support children, exploring:

how poverty, adversity, and social, emotional and mental health all influence the developing child

the science behind play, and why it is so important for young children

how we can take ideas from different disciplines such as psychology and anthropology and interweave these with the overarching research of neuroscience

why adult interaction (both practitioner and parent/carer) with children is crucial for the developing brain

the importance of reflective practice to encourage readers to consider their actions and develop their understanding of important topics raised in the book.

With a wealth of case studies and reflective practices weaving throughout, readers will be encouraged and empowered to pause and consider their own practice. *Little Brains Matter* will be essential reading for anyone interested in early childhood development.

Debbie Garvey is an author, trainer, consultant, lecturer, researcher and facilitator. Debbie is a huge advocate of enabling and empowering the use and development of professional reflective practice in order to support quality experiences for children, families and staff. Debbie has particular research interests in developing understanding across the early childhood sector in regard to leadership, neuroscience, PSED/wellbeing, imposter syndrome, the work of Bronfenbrenner and the use of ethnography and autoethnography.

Little Minds Matter: Promoting Social and Emotional Wellbeing in the Early Years

Series Advisor: Sonia Mainstone-Cotton

The *Little Minds Matter* series promotes best practice for integrating social and emotional health and wellbeing into the early years setting. It introduces practitioners to a wealth of activities and resources to support them in each key area: from providing access to ideas for unstructured, imaginative outdoor play; activities to create a sense of belonging and form positive identities; and, importantly, strategies to encourage early years professionals to create a workplace that positively contributes to their own wellbeing, as well as the quality of their provision. The *Little Minds Matter* series ensures that practitioners have the tools they need to support every child.

Supporting the Wellbeing of Children with SEND
Essential Ideas for Early Years Educators
Kerry Payne

Supporting Behaviour and Emotions in the Early Years
Strategies and Ideas for Early Years Educators
Tamsin Grimmer

A Guide to Mental Health for Early Years Educators
Putting Wellbeing at the Heart of Your Philosophy and Practice
Kate Moxley

Supporting the Wellbeing of Children with EAL
Essential Ideas for Practice and Reflection
Liam Murphy

Building Positive Relationships in the Early Years
Conversations to Empower Children, Professionals, Families and Communities
Sonia Mainstone-Cotton and Jamel Carly Campbell

Developing Child-Centred Practice for Safeguarding and Child Protection
Strategies for Every Early Years Setting
Rachel Buckler

Little Brains Matter
A Practical Guide to Brain Development and Neuroscience in Early Childhood
Debbie Garvey

Creativity and Wellbeing in the Early Years
Practical Ideas and Activities for Young Children
Sonia Mainstone-Cotton

Anti-Racist Practice in the Early Years
A Holistic Framework for the Wellbeing of All Children
Valerie Daniel

A Practical Guide to Brain Development and Neuroscience in Early Childhood

Debbie Garvey

Routledge
Taylor & Francis Group

LONDON AND NEW YORK

Designed cover image: Zach

First published 2023
by Routledge
4 Park Square, Milton Park, Abingdon, Oxon OX14 4RN

and by Routledge
605 Third Avenue, New York, NY 10158

Routledge is an imprint of the Taylor & Francis Group, an informa business

© 2023 Debbie Garvey

The right of Debbie Garvey to be identified as author of this work has been asserted in accordance with sections 77 and 78 of the Copyright, Designs and Patents Act 1988.

British Library Cataloguing-in-Publication Data
A catalogue record for this book is available from the British Library

Library of Congress Cataloging-in-Publication Data
Names: Garvey, Debbie, author.
Title: Little brains matter: a practical guide to brain development and neuroscience in early childhood/Debbie Garvey.
Description: First Edition. | New York: Routledge, 2023. | Includes bibliographical references and index. |
Summary: Provided by publisher.
Identifiers: LCCN 2022042625 (print) | LCCN 2022042626 (ebook) | ISBN 9780367724474 (Hardback) | ISBN 9780367724467 (Paperback) | ISBN 9781003154846 (eBook)
Subjects: LCSH: Cognitive learning. | Cognitive neuroscience. | Cognition in children. | Early childhood education. | Education, Primary.
Classification: LCC LB1062 .G398 2023 (print) | LCC LB1062 (ebook) | DDC 155.4/13–dc23/eng/20221019
LC record available at https://lccn.loc.gov/2022042625
LC ebook record available at https://lccn.loc.gov/2022042626

ISBN: 978-0-367-72447-4 (hbk)
ISBN: 978-0-367-72446-7 (pbk)
ISBN: 978-1-003-15484-6 (ebk)

DOI: 10.4324/9781003154846

Typeset in Optima
by Deanta Global Publishing Services, Chennai, India

This book is dedicated to all the adults who loved and supported young children throughout the global pandemic of Covid-19.

Know that you made a difference – everyday.

On behalf of the children of the world – Thank You!

I would not have finished this book without help, support, challenge, and encouragement from so many other people. Please know, I could not have done this without all of you:

Zach (aged 6), thank you for talking to me about what helps children to feel loved, "grownups that listen, have fun and play, family, friends, being outside, cuddles and sunshine", and for drawing the front cover picture to explain.

Clare Ashworth, senior editor at Speechmark and Sonia Mainstone-Cotton, Little Minds Matter series advisor – thank you for calming me through the chaos, reading copious re-writes, and always providing perceptive and supportive feedback.

Leah Burton, Molly Kavanagh, and Rachel Cook – my thanks to everyone in the fabulous 'back stage' team who have made the production of this book so enjoyable – any errors that remain are my mine.

Gill Holden, Andrea Layzell, Rachael Singleton, Sarah Watkins and Sarah Collins – your support, encouragement and friendship have enabled me to simultaneously manage this book, the MA, and the last two years. I am blessed that you are part of my life.

Dr Nathan Archer, Dr Yinka Olusoga and Dr Julie Ovington – thank you for listening to my ramblings, generously sharing your knowledge and insights, supporting me to be brave, and facilitating courageous conversations.

Joanna Ainsworth, Liz Clarke, and Kelly Miguel Hidalgo, thank you for so generously sharing your time, proofreading, and offering encouraging and insightful comments.

Julie Denton, Kelly Roberts, Pauline Scott, Carey and Leroy – thank you for your warmth and generosity in sharing your reflections for the case studies.

MG – for over 35 years you have been by my side. I would not be where I am, or contemplating the next step, without your unwavering support, love, and belief. Thank you.

And finally – all of you – thank you for reading this book –

I'd love to know what you think!

This book – *Little Brains Matter: A Practical Guide to Brain Development and Neuroscience in Early Childhood* – is the latest in our Little Minds Matter series. This is a crucial book in our series. Within the early years, we all need to have an understanding of brain development and neuroscience, but sometimes this can be a mind-boggling area to understand unless you have a background in it! In this book, Debbie aims to demystify the area; she opens up the subject by explaining and putting the knowledge into practice that we will all be familiar with.

Throughout *Little Brains Matter*, Debbie weaves in case studies, examples, and reflective exercises, giving us space to link what we are reading with the children we work with. An important element of the book is the space it gives us to reflect, question, consider and ponder over. I feel this is a book to be read over time; one to come back to, read a section, think about it, reflect on it and then read some more. There is so much depth to this book, it will keep on adding to our knowledge the more we read it.

The title of the book tells us it is a practical guide, and this is such an important aspect of the book as it offers practical ways to apply what we have read and embed this into our practice. I would suggest this is a book that settings could use in team meetings as part of an ongoing continuing professional development program – there are many reflective questions that teams could use to think about their practice. This will also be an incredibly useful book if you are studying early childhood studies, giving you a vital foundational knowledge to neuroscience and brain development.

I hope you enjoy reading this book. I know it is one I am going to continue to revisit and will be using the reflective questions in my work and with the teams I support.

Sonia Mainstone-Cotton
Series Advisor
August 2022

For some time now my work, training and writing has fluttered around the edges of neuroscience and brain development. My previous books have touched on some of the research and theory currently being developed across the globe. With this book I am excited to delve into this area in a broader way.

When I consider my 35-plus years' career, the discussions we are having now about neuroscience and brain development are among the most exciting. When I reflect on these decades of practice, I know that the science we are only just beginning to understand is helping to give confidence and credibility to many of the early childhood practices we *know* to be right. By that, I mean things such as how we have always known that being outdoors is good for children (and adults too for that matter), but now – *science* is showing us why that is true.

What I think is clear, is that theory, science, and practice are interwoven, or to clarify, they *should* be interwoven. What I hope we will do throughout this book is encourage and empower the early childhood sector to confidently explore the science and research and consider how we can weave this into our practice with young children.

Language

It might be helpful here to have just a few words on language. Writing a book means we have to make some decisions about the language we use; for example, it doesn't make sense to always write parents/carers or practitioners/teachers. Therefore, if it is OK with you, can we agree the following:

as we progress through the book, and use one of these words or phrases – we agree that we are using the meaning in the widest sense of the word(s).

Children: means any child of any age – babies, young children, older children and so on. It also means children with a range of abilities, from a range of backgrounds, families, cultures, etc. As you read, think about the children you work with, have worked with, or might work with in the future.

Adults/Grownups: can be parents, carers, foster carers, grandparents, aunties, uncles, adult siblings, practitioners, childminders, teachers, cooks, cleaners, gardeners, other staff, and so on – a whole host of people that children come into contact with.

Leaders/Managers: leadership and management are used interchangeably and mean anyone with some form of leadership or management responsibility.

Me, Myself and I: you, we and us are used throughout. Sometimes I am talking about me, or you and that should make sense. But mainly I am talking about us – this is a journey we are exploring together.

ECCE: Early Childhood Care and Education is far too long to read and type. Plus, there are several versions referring to early years or early childhood – so ECCE or 'early childhood' are simply my preferred ways.

Setting: there are so many words to describe where children are in terms of professional ECCE provision. These include daycare, nursery, kindergarten, nursery school, reception class, childminder, pre-school, playgroup, out of school provision, full day, sessional, full time, part time and many other variations. The words 'setting', 'provision' and 'childcare'/'school' are used throughout, and should be taken in the widest sense of the words.

Reflective Practice: these are a range of reflective exercises, scenarios and so on – opportunities to pause and think. These exercises are designed to encourage reflection, it is not about right or wrong answers, it is about considering the research and thinking through how it might apply in everyday practice. The reflective exercises are there to help and support – you can scribble in the book, or jot notes elsewhere. Please note: The reflective practice exercises are developed to support thinking – they are not intended to represent any specific person or situation.

Case Studies: there are several case studies included in this book. These are written by practitioners, who have kindly shared their thoughts and reflections on an area of practice. Some names have been anonymised by request, but all words and scenarios discussed are genuine.

If Not, Why Not: is a question I use a lot – it isn't meant to be a criticism. It is just a 'pause for thought', a suggestion to just stop and have a think. This also links with the 'why do we do that', or the 'so what' questions. Do we stop and pause to consider if what we are doing is still 'fit for purpose', useful, relevant and takes on board the latest research-informed practices and thinking?

Using This Book: this is *your* book, and how you use it will affect how useful it is. For example, don't feel you have to start at the beginning and work through to the end – start wherever your interest is. In other words – make this book work for you.

And finally, at times we all find we need to 'Take A Moment'. As you wander through this book there may be some things that are difficult to read and think about. – My thanks to Sonia Mainstone-Cotton for permission to reproduce this.

TAKE A MOMENT

It may bring up strong feelings in you about children you work with or have worked with. It could also bring up feelings and emotions in relation to your children, or your childhood. Your wellbeing is crucial. Whilst you are reading this book, I would like you to be mindful about the feelings it is raising in you. Be kind to yourself. If you are finding this difficult or triggering, take some time to nurture yourself. This might be by making yourself a cup of tea, doing some meditation, spending some time outdoors, or speaking to someone you trust.

(Mainstone-Cotton 2021:8)

After all, looking after our own wellbeing and making sure our brains are OK is crucial if we are to support healthy brain development in children.

The 'Little Minds Matter' series from Speechmark publications, part of Routledge Education, seems a natural home for a book about brain development. In particular, brains that belong to babies and children of all ages. Of course, we cannot talk about neuroscience and brain development in young children without considering the brains of the grownups around them – so we will explore some of that too.

The world is becoming more aware of the impact of early brain development and neuroscience in relation to young children. The science surrounding this is moving at an astonishing rate, and the knowledge this brings is fascinating. However, it would also be true to say that neuroscience has become a bit of a 'buzz' word over the last few years – with a great many opposing views. This can mean that things get a little confusing at times. Throughout this book, I hope we will embark on a practical, reflective journey together and explore what is useful, what is relevant, and how the science can help in early childhood practice.

I am a strong believer in gathering information from a range of sources to help us in our practical day-to-day work with children and families. It can be useful to look to other professions, which often offer thinking and ideas that can be different, but complementary to our own. As we move through the book, we will consider the most recent, cutting-edge science, theory, and research from across the world, and from a range of professions. This is designed to be a practical book, and wherever possible uses simplified versions of the science for us to explore in ways that make sense to us in early childhood.

Each chapter has, at the end, a bibliography. In the bibliography you will find the references for the direct quotes in that chapter (in brackets), but also other books, texts, information, videos, and websites, etc., that I have found useful along the way. Throughout the book are references, and names in brackets. Some references are attached to direct quotes and will have page numbers. References in brackets with names and dates are suggestions for starting points for further reading, usually I have included one or two to get you started. I urge you to explore the bibliographies – in here you will find a treasure trove of further resources to support your Continuing Professional Development (CPD). Some will be well loved and respected, some obscure. Some you will know; some will offer new knowledge or offer opportunity for reflection. My reading and researching behind my books is always eclectic. It brings me great joy to put together a list of evidenced-based, research-informed resources that can support us as reflective early childhood professionals – I hope you find them useful too.

The Journey?

It might be useful to share a little of my journey, and how I developed an interest in neuroscience. It has been a journey of over 35 years, but one that has had a particular focus for the last 15 years. My journey into neuroscience was not originally about learning and development – that came later, with the realisation that stressed, worried or frightened brains cannot learn (or at least are going to find learning much more difficult). I have written elsewhere about bringing up two abandoned kittens (Garvey, 2018) and how that raised my interest in personal, social, and emotional development (PSED) in humans. This led to further research into emotional development and wellbeing in particular. This, in turn, led to exploring how emotions respond to hormones and how the brain is involved in that process.

This book is an accumulation of my reading, research, experiences, knowledge and understanding. Writing this book has developed my knowledge and understanding further, and continues to do so. I hope you will enjoy continuing the journey with me.

Initially, we will set the scene on the wide-ranging sciences under the neuroscience umbrella. As we move on, we will consider some of the research in this area, and in addition explore why play is vital to healthy brain development. As we progress on this journey of exploration, we will look at how environments influence children, and how sometimes, albeit inadvertently, we actually make life difficult for children. There will be opportunities to reflect on how poverty, and social, emotional and mental health and so on, influence the developing child. We will also explore the role of adults, and how we need to ensure we reflect on our approaches to early childhood.

One of the things I have found increasingly useful throughout my career, is the opportunity for reflection. Those moments when I was supported to just stop and think, those times when I could jot down some thoughts, or just have a chat with a trusted colleague, for example. One of the things I am told that people like about my books, is how there are many opportunities to pause and reflect. As we progress through the book, we will have reflection points – exercises, case studies, scenarios, and reflective questions, for example. I hope that you will find them as useful as I do, as an opportunity to just 'pause' and consider practice. (And remember to think about the things that are going well too.)

Ultimately, this is *your* book, so make it work for you – write on it, jot notes in the margins, or talk to a trusted colleague about the things we discuss. More than anything, I hope we recognise the importance of stopping for a moment and just thinking about what we do, and why we do it.

Throughout the book, we will be able to consider how our practices around areas such as the environment, play, interactions, and wellbeing support healthy brain development. We will consider how each of these are important in their own right, how they are interlinked, and how difficulties in one area will inevitably impact on others. As we move towards the end, I hope that together we will be enabled, encouraged and empowered to reflect on the journey. I hope we will have the confidence to develop our own 'practitioner research' and continue to use the evidenced-based research, theory, and science to add to our own knowledge, experience and understanding in order to offer the very best experiences for children, their families and our colleagues.

It can be really helpful when starting out on a journey of discovery to begin by defining what we are actually looking for (or at). The trouble is, neuroscience can be such a difficult word to define, and it can seem that everyone has their own (and possibly different) definitions. If we look at a straightforward dictionary definition, the Cambridge dictionary offers:

> The scientific study of the nervous system and the brain.
>
> (www.dictionary.cambridge.org, 2022)

A wider definition from King's College London's School of Neuroscience, Institute of Psychiatry, Psychology and Neuroscience talks about:

> At its most basic, neuroscience is the study of the nervous system – from structure to function, development to degeneration, in health and in disease. It covers the whole nervous system, with a primary focus on the brain.
>
> (www.kcl.ac.uk/neuroscience, 2022)

Meanwhile, words describing associated fields of science, study, and research, such as neurophysiology, physiology, psychology, chemistry, biochemistry, biology, and molecular biology, etc., pop up on a regular basis. These are often joined by terms such as cognitive neuroscience, educational neuroscience, behavioural neuroscience, developmental neuroscience, computational neuroscience and so on… That's before we start talking about the technology and language around neuroimaging, in other words, the machines and associated knowledge that allow us to physically look at (and inside) brains, as we try to develop our

DOI: 10.4324/9781003154846-1

understanding of what brains do. This includes areas such as radiology, photography, x-ray, and ultrasound, for example. Then there is a whole host of abbreviations, acronyms and initialisms such as MRI, fMRI, MEG, EEG, NIRS and PET scans.

And at that point it would be completely understandable to switch off and go make a cup of tea! Whilst it would normally be expected and would also be fairly easy now to make a big, long list of what all these words and terms mean, this isn't a dictionary, and I guess it wouldn't make for very exciting reading. Instead, some of these terms are spread throughout the book and we will explore them in relation to practice – where, hopefully, they will make more sense. (Or you can always explore some of the items in the bibliography, where these and many more terms are explained.)

The issue we have when there are so many terms, is that potentially everyone has a different understanding. If I use the phrase of a 'perfect evening' as an example – everyone could have a very different understanding of what that looks and feels like. The same can happen with 'neuroscience' – depending on where we are looking or who we are talking to. Whilst this might not be too much of a problem, my concern is that we could then ignore some areas of science and research that could be really helpful. Also, it can simply become just a ridiculously complicated debate that focusses too much on where things 'should' fit. All of this does nothing to encourage participation with the very people who are engaged with little brains every day – parents, grandparents, families, practitioners, nurses, teachers, lunchtime staff, sports coaches, health visitors, childminders, foster carers, playworkers, students, social workers, and anyone else who spends time with young children. In other words, the very people who have the biggest impact in shaping and supporting young children's brains – the research needs to be accessible to all.

So, I think it might be useful for those of us who are interested in why little brains matter, and/or are engaged in any part of this wonderful period of early childhood, to start with a definition that makes sense to us. We will, of course, ensure we still acknowledge other terms and associated fields. For me, this one is particularly helpful:

Neuroscience has traditionally been classed as a subdivision of biology. These days, it is an *interdisciplinary* science which liaises closely with other disciplines, such as mathematics, linguistics, engineering, computer science, chemistry, philosophy, psychology, and medicine.

(Nordqvist, 2016 [no page], *emphasis added*)

It very much feels that this is an umbrella term, or an over-arching definition, that allows us to embrace any, and all, areas of research and science that are interested in growth and development. This wider definition also means we can consider a whole host of areas that might be able to help and support us in our work with young children. Furthermore, this definition encourages us to consider the holistic nature of our work not just with children, but also families, colleagues, communities and so on, and explore the range of research and science that is important for supporting wider understanding of neuroscience in relation to us as *humans*. Let's consider this a little:

REFLECTIVE PRACTICE
Thinking about Neuroscience

Consider the discussion we have just had, then have a think about the following questions.

What does the term 'neuroscience' mean to you?
Your colleagues? Your team? Others around you?
How can we support everyone to understand and use the term 'neuroscience' confidently in its very widest sense?
How can we ensure that we include (and embrace) a range of research, theory, studies, debates and sciences to influence our understanding?
How can we ensure that we encompass all areas that are interested in human growth and development?
How can we ensure that neuroscience is understood as being wide ranging, *with* a particular interest in the development of the brain?

And, in terms of all of the questions:

What might help?
Who could help?

3

Where could you look/start?
Why – why do you think that? (And if not, why not?)
Anything else you can think of/want to add?

You might want to jot down some notes.

Hopefully, your reflections have helped to clarify how you feel and think, and possibly offered some areas for further reflection or areas to explore. In terms of developing our early childhood understanding, and ensuring that little brains *do* matter, let's proceed with these questions in mind.

Biologically Speaking

Human babies arrive in the world wholly reliant on, as well as needing and expecting to be cared for, nurtured, and supported by other (bigger) humans. It is now widely agreed that the reason human babies are very underdeveloped at birth is down to the birth process. It is all about size – the longer a baby is in the womb, the harder it is for a mother to nourish it! Likewise, if babies were any bigger, then getting out into the big, wide world would be a much 'bigger' problem! This would not be great for mum (ouch!) – but also, it wouldn't be great for baby either. Therefore, in order to survive the birthing process, human babies *have* to be smaller. This means human babies arrive in the world very tiny in relation to their eventual size, and with no way of being able to defend themselves (Dunsworth and Eccleston, 2015; Rosenberg and Trevathan, 2002; Schultz, 1949; Wells et al., 2012).

The fact that babies expect to be cared for by 'grownups' is not exclusive to the human world. Many young animals are cared for by adults until they are of an age where they can fend for themselves. What is unusual is the length of time human offspring are cared for.

In the animal kingdom, parental responsibility is often relatively short-lived. Dependent on the species, baby birds, for example, stay in the nest for around 3–10 weeks. Baby leopards stay with their mother until around 2 years old, whilst male elephants usually leave the herd from around 10 years of age. The difference is the rate of growth if we consider that many other mammals can walk at a few hours old (think of those videos of wobbly deer, giraffes, and piglets), and most birds can fly at just a few weeks. A study (Stynoski et al., 2014) found that the female brightly coloured poison dart frog supplies her offspring with poison, so they become poisonous as they grow and develop. In other words, all of these babies grow and develop at a rapid rate, and that gives them some form of defensive mechanism from any potential predators. Almost from birth, the deer, giraffes, and piglets, etc., can run away, the birds can fly away, and the poison dart frog is so brilliantly, brightly coloured as a first warning of danger, which if ignored is likely to lead to instant death!

Whilst many animal species have brilliantly clever and evolved mechanisms for the protection of their young, what they perhaps do not have is the brilliantly clever and evolved capacity of the human brain. Whilst human babies are very advanced in some ways (and we will come back to that later), in other ways they are very underdeveloped.

Briefly Beginning with Brains

Although human brains are the most evolved on the planet, infinitely capable as they grow, human babies' brains are amongst the most underdeveloped at birth. In very simplified terms, the brain is a network of neurons, and neurons are just another name for brain cells. Brain cells are mainly formed before birth, and furthermore, at birth, not all brain cells are quite where they need to be. Some need to migrate to other parts of the brain and have to take quite long and treacherous journeys to get to their final destinations (Paredes et al., 2016). (Which might be worth bearing in mind when we are thinking about children born prematurely.)

Neurons are determined to communicate. Individual cells communicate with each other through synapses (or circuits). Over time, the more the synapses are used, the stronger they become. In other words, the more times we do something the stronger the connections become. You have probably experienced this when you are learning a new skill, it gets easier the more you do it. That is the connections in your brain working faster because they remember what has gone before. Synapses that aren't used are naturally 'pruned' away, as they are no longer needed.

(If you want to explore this more, the Center on the Developing Child at Harvard University has a range of resources on its website, and I would urge you to explore it further – see bibliography.)

In addition, neurons (brain cells) have 'arms', known as axons:

> A long arm called an axon allows the neuron to send information, in the form of an electrical signal … to other neurons, which can be quite far away in a different part of the brain.
>
> (Dumontheil and Mareschal, 2020: 23)

We also have glial cells which in effect are caretakers or engineers. Glial cells look after the "nutrients, maintenance, … cell repair, removal of damaged or infected neurons or synapses" (Dumontheil and Mareschal, 2020: 24). The glial (caretaker/engineer) cells also help by covering the axons (the long arms) in layers of a lipid, or fatty substance, known as myelin. This myelin sheath (covering) acts like insulation and allows information/messages to travel (or be processed) much faster.

In previous conversations with Professor Lynda Erskine, Chair in Development Neurobiology at the University of Aberdeen, Prof. Erskine talked of the importance of myelination:

> Many nerves in the body do not become fully myelinated until well into childhood. So [myelination is] important in young children as information may not pass from brain to e.g. muscles as fast as in adults, so [children] will be less co-ordinated etc.
>
> (Professor L. Erskine, 2016, personal communication, 14 November)

In other words, myelination speeds up messages moving between areas within the brain, and to other parts of the body. In some cases, the messages will travel faster, because the myelination process is well underway. In other situations, the messages in children's bodies and brains may take longer to travel around as the myelination process is not as advanced.

Forbes and Gallo (2017: 579) discuss how myelination needs specific elements to develop. Positive, rich, and stimulating physical and emotional environments support myelination, whereas negative influences can inhibit myelination:

> Newness, challenge, exercise, diet, and love... without these five essentials, an organism may lose the ability to carry out basic motor and cognitive functions.

A really simple example would be that a child who has been supported to have lots of experience of climbing trees will have more knowledge and understanding about 'trees' and 'climbing' than a child who has never climbed a tree. This means that messages (information) about 'trees' and 'climbing' will travel around the brain and body quicker. Therefore, the experienced tree climber has knowledge and understanding and can use already present skills, build on those skills and develop new ones. And build on and develop further understanding and knowledge along the way. It becomes a repeated (or cyclical) process – the more we do something the more we understand it, and (hopefully) the better we get at it.

REFLECTIVE PRACTICE

Myelination Messages?

Let's consider some scenarios that are likely to be very familiar to early childhood professionals:

> Billie is 9 months old and starting to use furniture to try to stand up, although not yet crawling. Dad mentions that Billie likes being in the pushchair or the highchair. Billie's mum has had bouts of depression.

Jared is 18 months old. Jared loves bikes and anything with wheels. One day, a delivery of new outdoor toys arrives, and there is a new bike. The bike has two seats and needs two children to work together to be able to ride it.

Shabnam is nearly 3 and enjoys anything to do with painting and gluing. Shabnam's mum tells you that over the weekend they have been using dad's mobile phone to take photographs of Shabnam's artwork to send to extended members of the family. Shabnam has a hearing impairment.

Grygoriy is 4 years old. Grygoriy's family has recently arrived in the U.K. as asylum seekers. The family is waiting to hear about its refugee status. Grygoriy seems to like being outside, especially playing football, and stays close to an adult.

Using your professional knowledge, and experiences of children you know or work with (now or previously), think about the range of circumstances children live in, and the range of experiences children have. Then consider the children in the scenarios. Reflect on which areas of development the children may have strongly myelinated pathways in (or not). How might the children's early experiences potentially influence the following areas of development:

Physically?
Socially?
Emotionally?

	Myelinated pathways	Unmyelinated or less myelinated pathways
Physical Development (e.g., coordination, posture, abilities, etc.)		

Social Development (e.g., relationships, connections, abilities, etc.)		
Emotional Development (e.g., behaviours, feelings, abilities, etc.)		
Any other thoughts/comments:		

You might want to jot down a few thoughts in the grid.

Hopefully your reflections should show how myelination (or lack of myelination) can influence development. In addition, it should be apparent when and where children may need more time to think, or extra support in order to achieve something. A child with a difficult home life, or who has a disability, or has been unwell, or is stressed being in new surroundings, might need longer to process the messages between brain and body, or extra support from a trusted adult, in order to develop the skills, knowledge, experience and understanding needed.

In the busyness of the world, it can be all too easy to forget that we all have different starting points, different experiences and have had, and are on, different journeys – all of which influence our brains, bodies, and behaviours. We often do not take these things into consideration. For example, how often do we communicate something (either to children or to grown-ups) where we *expect* them to know something, be able to do something, or be able to give an answer – just because it is something we know or can do?

9

In other words, do we give children (and indeed adults) the time to think and process? Time to ask questions? Time to find further information and so on? And, if we don't, is it any wonder that children (and indeed adults) at times display distressed behaviours?

Cellular Communication?

Let's try and think of this in another way. Think about New Year's Eve. Every year millions of people around the world want to send thoughts and wishes to friends and family. When we send a photo, an email, or a message, some will be delivered instantly, others may take a while. Also, the communication networks have 'caretakers' who help to unscramble all the pieces of data and information coming in, and then make sure these get to the correct recipient. If something goes wrong, the communication networks then send 'engineers' to sort out the issues… Some issues will be sorted quickly, and no one will notice, and some messages will take a lot longer to get where they need to be than others. This is very similar to sending information, messages, and communication between cells in the body.

For our bodies and brains to function, we constantly analyse thousands of pieces of data and information. Messages travel throughout our bodies, all areas communicating with each other – from the tips of our fingers and toes to the very top of our heads.

Let's look at this from a sending a message point of view. In very simplified terms:

1. A message is sent – which can be from either an internal or external source. Internal messages come from a cell somewhere in the body (such as inside an organ or a muscle), or external messages come via one or more of the five senses – so we see, smell, hear, taste and/or touch something.
2. The message is carried from its starting point through a network of 'pathways' which connect the muscles, organs, and senses, and is known as the Peripheral Nervous System (PNS).
3. Then on into the Central Nervous System (CNS), the message travels up the spinal column and finally into the brain.

4. The message is then carried to the correct part (or parts) of the brain – where a decision can then be made on how to respond or react, ask for more information, or send information back, for example.

All of this usually happens in a fraction of a second. Some of the decisions we are completely unaware of – such as the ones that cause us to sneeze or feel hungry or to pull our hand away from a hot oven. Others, we are acutely aware of, and we are actively involved in the decisions the brain makes, such as when to blow our noses, or what to eat for lunch, for example. Or – at least they are for us as adults – because we have had previous experiences of these things. For children, it will depend on previous experiences, and levels of myelination.

Brain Exploration: Cortex, Cerebellum or Cerebral?

Now we have explored the tiniest pieces of the brain (neurons and brain cells), let's look at some of the areas. Travelling up the spinal column, the first part of the brain we meet is the brainstem (sometimes written as two words – brain stem, and sometimes called the hindbrain). This part of the brain is vitally important for bodily functions, reflexes, alertness, and sleep, amongst other things. Damage to the brainstem is thought to play a part in both Chronic Fatigue Syndrome/Myalgic Encephalomyelitis (CFS/ME) and Long-Covid.

If we move into the 'middle part' of the brain (sometimes called the midbrain), often referred to as the 'emotion centre', then we come across words such as:

Amygdala (meaning almond shaped).
Hippocampus (the Latin name for seahorse is Hippocampus which means 'Horse Caterpillar' – this area of the brain is vaguely seahorse shaped).
Hypothalamus (which sits under the thalamus; hypo – meaning under, and thalamus – meaning chamber).

This is the area of the brain associated with emotion, memory, and, interestingly, also with processing information in relation to the sense of smell.

Then finally, we move into the 'cortex', the upper/front part of the brain (sometimes called the forebrain), often referred to as the highly evolved area, where learning and thinking happens. Here we have words such as cortex (Latin for bark – meaning the 'outer part'), cerebral or cerebrum, and neocortex (neo – meaning new, as it is the newest part of the evolution process).

There are also other related words such as the cerebellum (near the brainstem), which is associated with balance, muscles, and movement, as well as words including hemispheres and lobes, which are simply terms for different parts of the brain.

It may be that there are terms here that are more familiar or feel more comfortable to use. Likewise, it may be that there are terms that are unfamiliar, and you may want to explore the bibliography for ideas on where to look for more explanations. For the purposes of my writing, the following seems to work:

> I am also conscious that many of us interested in early childhood are not scientists (me included), but we have to have some language we can use, without overcomplicating the subject. Therefore, it is with this understanding in mind, that I will use the terms:
>
> the brainstem (sometimes referred to as the reptilian brain)
> the limbic brain (sometimes referred to as the mammalian brain)
> the neocortex.
>
> (Garvey, 2018: 34)

Reticular Activating System

In addition, there is one more term I would like us to explore – the Reticular Activating System (RAS), sometimes referred to as the Reticular Formation. The RAS is a network of neural connections found in the brainstem. In very simple terms, the RAS, amongst other things, plays a part in sleep/wakefulness, pain control, heartrate, and motor coordination – including how we combine different areas of the body to cause movement.

Furthermore, the RAS plays a role in filtering information. An example of this is when we are scared or worried. The human brain finds it hard to differentiate between a very big threat and a small threat – how we react is pretty much the same until we know the danger has gone and we are safe again. We will have all had those days where we find it really difficult to concentrate because we have something praying on our mind. That's the RAS trying to get us to only concentrate on what it sees as a threat or danger – no matter how small. Incidentally, this can also be a real worry, or an imagined one – so worrying about something that might or could happen – no matter how ludicrous or ridiculous that worry might be.

It is also worth noting here that hormones play a part in how our brains work (or don't as the case may be):

> Designed to regulate and control various functions of the body, humans have around 50 hormones, and these are controlled by a group of glands. Hormones include cortisol, oxytocin, thyroxine, insulin, adrenaline, dopamine, serotonin, oestrogen and testosterone, to name just a few. Each of these hormones plays a specific role, and you may well have personal experiences of how the body reacts when they do not do the job they are designed for.
>
> (Garvey, 2018: 48)

When we feel safe, loved, and cared for, hormones such as oxytocin, dopamine and serotonin are produced. On the other hand, cortisol and adrenaline are released when we feel stressed, worried, or anxious.

> In humans (and indeed in mammals), when feeling stressed, frightened, worried or scared or similar (in other words, when feeling threatened), the hormone cortisol is released. A small amount of cortisol is good for the brain; it supports the effort needed to persevere and to reach goals and so on, such as when feeling slightly stressed/pressured to meet a tight deadline. However, in large quantities, cortisol is toxic to the human brain, and therefore in times of great stress, the RAS filter steps in to protect the rest of the brain from being overloaded with a toxic substance. In effect, this means that the RAS filter shuts down access to the rest of the brain, acting as a gatekeeper or drawbridge, or imagine a net-like cluster that 'catches' useless or irrelevant information. This is an unconscious act, … enables the body, and … brain, to concentrate on

what is causing the threat. Only information in relation to the threat is allowed through. No other information is processed, and cortisol is prevented from poisoning the rest of the brain. This in turn allows the brain to concentrate and decide on a course of action – fight, flight or freeze.

(Garvey, 2018: 49)

Studies have shown that the RAS appears to play a role in Post-Traumatic Stress Disorder (PTSD), where people have experienced very real danger. The RAS becomes overactive, and there is experience of exaggerated responses, hypersensitivity, and hypervigilance (increased alertness). This includes feelings of always being tense, or constantly on guard, or overtly aware of, or sensitive to, signs of threat or danger (Garcia-Rill, 2019).

Which brings us to why the RAS is important to our journey of exploring neuroscience in terms of early childhood – as it plays a role in the fight, flight or freeze response.

Fight or Flight or Freeze?

The fight, flight or freeze response is the body's way of preparing us to deal with danger, threats and/or predators. It is found in most animals and at a basic level is about survival instincts. Imagine you are a gazelle, grazing out on the savannah, when suddenly a gentle breeze brings with it the scent of a lion. Immediately, your heart will beat faster, your muscles will constrict and in a split second your brain will make a decision as to your best chances of survival. Am I bigger, stronger than the lion (fight)? Can I outrun the lion (flight)? Or... can I stay really still and really quiet and hope the lion walks straight past me, whilst I decide what to do next (freeze)?

This decision is accompanied by a series of messages communicating throughout the body, via the PNS we mentioned earlier. The PNS is divided into what is called the *somatic* nervous system and the *autonomic* nervous system. Somatic is usually associated with conscious or voluntary actions (something we decide we are going to do). Autonomic, as its name suggests, is about things that happen automatically.

Whilst many systems and areas within the body are engaged in the response to stress/danger, in terms of our gazelle (and indeed us as humans), it is the autonomic system we are most interested in for now. The autonomic system can be split even further – into the *sympathetic* and *parasympathetic* nervous systems:

The sympathetic system helps in preparing for stress/stressful situations.
The parasympathetic system brings everything back to normal afterwards.

Most of the time the two systems operate happily together and in harmony, keeping everything tickety-boo!

Back to our gazelle and the scent of the lion, which sends the sympathetic part of the autonomic nervous system into overdrive. Automatically, lots of things happen at once, as various systems and areas of the body prepare for what could happen. For example, the pupils dilate, heartrate and breathing change, any pain is repressed, and hormones are pumped throughout the body. The RAS does its job brilliantly here, and only allows information regarding the threat to be processed; everything else becomes irrelevant. All of these unconscious actions are designed to support the fight or flight response. These actions send signals and prepare the body in case fighting or running might be the only way to survive.

The freeze response is associated with being temporarily unable to move – literally 'frozen with fear'. In addition, the research suggests that the freeze response is usually a brake mechanism, or a pause, used before deciding what action to take (Hagenaars et al., 2014; Roelofs, 2017). This is often influenced by prior experience, understanding and/or knowledge. So, for our gazelle, this could be knowledge and experience of previously outrunning a lion, or knowledge of the area, and knowing where there are possible escape routes, for example.

Meanwhile, if our gazelle can see no way of escape, and the fear becomes so extreme as to be life-threatening, this can result in involuntary paralysis, or 'Tonic Immobility', sometimes referred to as TI (Bados et al., 2008; Fragkaki et al., 2016; Roelofs, 2017). In other words – lay down and play dead! This is the last stand, literally so frightened there is nowhere to turn. Often there is no sound (mutism), no feelings of pain (analgesia) as well as no movement, although uncontrollable shaking and trembling can be present.

The research on TI in animals is fairly conclusive, and the term 'playing possum' is common. Those of us with well-fed, but still 'hunter-at-heart' cats may have seen this in the poor mouse caught in the 'jaws of death'. Often, it is the toy mouse – but occasionally, the hunter takes over, and it is a real mouse that turns to TI as its only means of survival. Once dropped by the cat, the mouse lays there as if dead, literally catatonic, rigid, and incapable of movement.

No longer the hunter, the cat looks around nonchalantly, its claws now all safely sheathed. The cat extends a soft paw and prods the poor mouse a few times and when getting no reaction, soon bored, walks away! This leaves the mouse to almost miraculously appear to rise from the dead and regain the use of its legs, before being (hopefully, and hopefully swiftly) rescued by the long-suffering humans and carefully released back out into the wild. Slightly traumatised maybe, but alive none-the-less.

The research on TI in humans is gaining momentum:

> The body's stress response shifts into a mode of conserving physical resources … redirects the body's energies toward healing (the immune system) and staying alive rather than fight or flight.
>
> (Ford et al., 2015: 193)

> TI [Tonic Immobility] was indeed more present in those with sexual violence (childhood or adulthood), childhood emotional abuse, serious accidents, and war-related trauma.
>
> (Hagenaars, 2016: 251)

Which brings us back to children. All of this is worth thinking about when we consider some of the children we work with, and some of the experiences they may have sadly had in their very young lives. We will all, I am sure, have memories of the children who respond to real or perceived threats by moving into fight or flight mode. Likewise, we will all be able to recall supporting children who needed help to co-regulate and return their parasympathetic systems to normal. For me, it is the children who stand back, stay very quiet and hope no one will notice them that we should take extra care to notice. The children who respond to real or perceived threats with the freeze response are the children that I worry most about.

A Few More Fs??

Researching for my writing brings up all kinds of interesting threads. I love it when a thread takes me down a bizarre path that ultimately leads back to an interesting and highly relevant point. Back to the comment earlier about ensuring we embrace 'a range of research, theory, studies, debates and sciences to influence our understanding'. Some paths are highly academic from peer-reviewed journals perhaps, some are practice-led research by practitioners proven in their field, and some are blogs and articles written by interested people – one thing all the threads have in common, is that they are *all, always*, interesting. And, if they are interesting, then I think they are worthy of exploration.

One such thread took me down a 'rabbit warren' of Fs. There are now discussions and explorations taking place, considering whether, in addition to the fight, flight, and freeze (TI/Tonic Immobility) responses, other reactions should be included. Finding an original article is sometimes elusive, but it appears generally accepted that Dr Curtis Reisinger first suggested this in a New York magazine article (Heaney, 2017). The fact that this extends the F alliteration adds to the interest – Dr Reisinger suggested flood, fawn and fatigue as other threat/stress responses we should also be considering. Let's think about these in a little more detail:

Flooding: being flooded with emotions, the feeling of being completely overwhelmed. Perhaps experiencing a range of similar or related emotions, or even conflicting or opposing ones.

Fawning: as in submissive, or to give in or submit. Perhaps, on a small scale, this could be about simply not having the fight left to argue about something. In extreme circumstances perhaps this is about the hope of experiencing less danger, or less harm, or as some primitive instinct in the hope of improving the chances of survival?

Fawning could also possibly be linked to the research behind what is generally known as 'Stockholm Syndrome' (Bachand and Djak, 2018; Heghes and Schiopu, 2019). Often described as a coping strategy, 'Stockholm Syndrome' is the term used to describe self-preservation safety tactics, usually developed in a relationship borne out of the manipulation and abuse of power. Often the relationship revolves around a person(s) in power, isolating someone from support and safety, by conditioning, and victimisation. Kidnapping, hostage scenarios, and domestic abuse are examples of this. These would perhaps link with the idea of fawning – as a tactical way of keeping safe. Fatigue: the overwhelming feeling of being tired, exhausted, and drained. This isn't just needing an early night. This is the complete and utter exhaustion experienced when our brains and bodies have had enough. The research behind this one is wide and varied – everything from pregnancy and pre-birth, to young children, right through to the impact on older people. The general feeling is that this is related to hormones and impacts on blood pressure, cognitive abilities, decision making, eating behaviours and often leads to a whole host of other problems. (A quick internet search of 'stress and fatigue' should bring up plenty of places to explore.)

Although this might feel like a digression, there is a very good reason for including all of this in a book looking at why little brains matter. Researching all of this, exploring all of this, writing all of this section, considering all of this in the minutest of detail brings me back time and time again to the same conclusion:

This isn't just about baby animals and survival techniques. This isn't just about animals on the savannah. This isn't just about adults. This is about all animals who live on this wonderful planet we are lucky enough to call home. This is about animals. This is about humans. *And* this is about *all* humans – including children. Therefore, all of this is vital for our understanding of why neuroscience is important and why little brains matter. Let's look at this from an early childhood perspective:

REFLECTIVE PRACTICE
Early Childhood Perspectives

Let's reconsider some of the key points covered in this last section:

Babies are born needing and expecting care and support from adults.
Babies' brains are incomplete at birth.

Messages travel throughout the brain and body.
The five senses are important.
The RAS plays a role in fight, flight, and freeze responses.
There are possibly more Fs: flood, fawn, fatigue.

Think about children you know or have known in comparison to each of these statements.

What are your thoughts?
What springs to mind?
Where is your thinking going?

Ultimately, this is mainly about two things – adults and stress. In other words, as adults, we spend a great deal of time and effort creating welcoming and enriched spaces and environments for children, creating feelings of safety, and providing the care and support needed throughout early childhood (and we'll explore more of this over other chapters). Or we can create feelings of stress. Admittedly it may be inadvertent, accidental and/or unintentional – but stress it is.

Just to clarify, this is unequivocally not about any form of abuse – any safeguarding concerns should be dealt with immediately. Neither is this about criticising or berating ourselves (or anyone else). This is about those everyday early childhood experiences that unintentionally cause stress. We have all done things we later regret. We have all shouted a little loudly, spoken a little harshly or made a decision that did not really consider the consequences. This is about things that get lost in the busyness of a day. This is about not always stopping to consider a child's perspective, or point of view. This is about those 'because I said so' type moments.

I know this is not easy, I know this can make for uncomfortable reading. Remember, this is a journey we are on together, and some bits of a journey can be a little bumpy. As with any journey, to see the magnificent view from the top we first need to climb up the hill (I promise you it will be worth it – so stay with me). This is about exploring the latest science through an early childhood lens, and using it to consider how we, as adults, have an impact on little brains. In other words, how we help shape the magnificent view. Let's start by exploring what stress is.

Stress, Stressors and Support

What stress is (or isn't) is another one of those difficult to define terms. It's surprising that as with 'neuroscience' there is no fully agreed definition, but again, there are some useful pointers. MIND (the mental health charity) offers the following on its website (March 2022):

> Stress isn't a psychiatric diagnosis, but it's closely linked to your mental health in two important ways:
>
> Stress can cause mental health problems and make existing problems worse. For example, if you often struggle to manage feelings of stress, you might develop a mental health problem like anxiety or depression.
> Mental health problems can cause stress. You might find coping with the day-to-day symptoms of your mental health problem, as well as potentially needing to manage medication, health care appointments or treatments, can become extra sources of stress.
>
> (© Mind. This information is published in full at
> mind.org.uk [March 2022].)

In addition, stress can be mainly identified as caused by internal or external factors, known as stressors.

External Stressors, as their name suggests, are external to the body. So, things such as the temperature, and being too hot or too cold, as well as feelings about our physical and emotional environments, and whether they alleviate or exacerbate our stress levels. This includes relationships, friendships, family, school, and work life, but also things like noise and lighting levels. Life-changing events, such as a new baby, moving to a new house, divorce and bereavement, etc., are examples of external stress-ors. Seeing others who are stressed can also initiate a sympathetic stress response.

Internal Stressors are therefore clearly internal to the body, things such as illness, lack of sleep, lack of control and psychological problems, for example. Uncertainty, worry, anxiety, thoughts, feelings, imagination, and memories can all be classed as internal stressors.

Levels of Stress

Furthermore, there are 'degrees' of stress depending on the length, severity, and nature of the stressor:

> Stressors can be acute and minor, like the temporary pain from a bee sting, or they can be chronic and life threatening, such as a battle with cancer.
>
> (Breton, 2020: 1)

Not all stress is bad. It might seem counter-productive to say, but we all need a little stress in our lives - when it is short term. This kind of stress helps us to learn how to deal with challenges or focus and concentrate – helpful when we are trying to work to a tight deadline, for example. As we've mentioned, although it can be difficult to think about, we know children experience stress too. The Center on the Developing Child at Harvard University offers a very useful overview:

> **Positive stress response** – brief increase in heart rate, mild elevations in stress hormone levels.
>
> **Tolerable stress response** – serious, temporary stress responses, buffered by supportive relationships.
>
> **Toxic stress response** – prolonged activation of stress response systems in the absence of protective relationships.
>
> (Center on the Developing Child/Toxic Stress, 2022)

This is a very useful overview. And – here's the thing – stress is manageable, for grownups and children, if we have support!

Support and Stress

Think about those difficult times in your life when you felt stressed. Now think about the people around you – what helped (or didn't)? Actually, let's look at this in a little more detail:

REFLECTIVE PRACTICE

Stress, Stressors and Support

Think about a couple of times in your life when you felt stressed.

> One when you felt supported.
> One when you did not feel supported.

You don't have to think about 'big, scary' stress situations, unless of course you want to. Just a straightforward, 'normal' event that caused some stress – something along the lines of a job interview, or giving a talk, or conflicting deadlines of too many things to do and not enough time, for example.

Now think about the following:

> How did you feel?
> What did you notice happening inside your body?
> How did that make you feel?

Now think about the people around you:

> What did they do, or say, that *did* help?
> How did that make you feel?
> What did they not do, or not say, that *did* help?
> How did that make you feel?

And then on the flip side:

> What did they do, or say, that *didn't* help?
> How did that make you feel?

What did they not do, or not say, that *didn't* help?
How did that make you feel?

I am sure your recollections of thoughts and feelings, and what people around you did, or did not do, to help are very clear. It should also be very clear as to the role 'support' plays in managing stressful situations – and indeed, the flip side, how it feels when we are not supported. (See also Chapter 6.)

If we think about our own experiences, support can be many things, and can be offered in many ways. For example, support can be emotional (talking through thoughts and feelings, etc.), physical (holding a hand, or a hug, etc.) or even practical (like helping with the shopping, etc.). In other words, we, as adults, can *usually* work through the stressful times, as we *usually* have someone to support us.

This is incredibly helpful as this means we know:

What stress looks and feels like.
What helps and makes a difference (and indeed what does not).

And… that is hugely reassuring, as that means we can use this knowledge in our day-to-day lives.

Not Just for Grownups?

I am sure much of the discussion we have just had will serve as reminders of our own experiences, and many (if not all) of us will recognise these signs, symptoms, and feelings. We recognise the internal and external stressors, our reactions to them, and those feelings of whether we were supported, or not, as the case may be.

The thing we need to remember here is that, although it may be uncomfortable to consider, stress is something that happens to all humans. Stress is not just a grownup concept, construct, or condition. In addition, we also know that chronic stress causes an over-production of glucocorticoids (hormones such as cortisol), which damage neurons. Therefore, this is particularly important when we are thinking about the experiences that children may (or may not) have had.

So, as this is a book mainly about children, these descriptions of stress need to be considered in relation to children too. Let's explore this a little further:

REFLECTIVE PRACTICE

Stress and Children

First, consider the children you know, or have known. Think about the things they did and said, how they behaved, how they showed their emotions, thoughts, and feelings, etc.

Now, let's look at the six Fs:

Fight
Flight
Freeze
Fawn(ing)
Flood(ing)
Fatigue

As you read these words, it will probably be fairly easy for you to think of times when you have seen children experiencing these stress responses, even in small ways.

Now, in more detail, go through each 'F' in turn. Can you come up with some examples of what you see, hear, notice, etc., when children are experiencing these stress responses?

Now consider:

How do the adults usually respond?
Why do you think that is?
Are there things that could be done differently?
Anything else?

I am fairly certain that you will be able to think of examples of all the six Fs. As people interested in early childhood, people who live and work with young children every day, I am sure the responses to stress are all too familiar. Maybe what needs to become more familiar is that we *see* them as responses to stress. Maybe we, as adults, need to consider what has caused that stress response in a child. Is it something we have helped with, or not, as the case may be? Is it a response to an internal or external stressor? Is it the environment – physical or emotional? And… we'll explore all of this (and more) in the next chapter.

Chapter Reflection

Thinking back over this chapter, consider the various elements (sections, quotes, reflective exercises, terminology, etc.). Are there any elements that:

Were particularly useful?
Need re-reading, or more thought or reflection?
You want to look up and/or explore further?

Any other thoughts or reflections?

Bibliography

The following are books, articles, web pages, organisations, documents, etc. that I have found useful (online versions, all accessed 20 July 2022). Some are directly referenced in this chapter – some are included as valuable sources of background reading that might be helpful. See also web resources at the end of Chapter 1.

Bachand, C. and Djak, N. (2018) Stockholm syndrome in athletics: a paradox. *Journal of Children Australia*, 43(3), pp. 175–180. Available at: https://doi.org/10.1017/cha.2018.31.

Bados, A., Toribio, L. and García-Grau, E. (2008) Traumatic events and tonic immobility. *Spanish Journal of Psychology*, 11(2), pp. 516–521. Available at: https://doi.org/10.1017/S1138741600004510.

Barnden, L. R., Shan, Z. Y., Staines, D. R., Marshall-Gradisnik, S., Finegan, K., Ireland, T. and Bhuta, S. (2019) Intra brainstem connectivity is impaired in chronic fatigue syndrome. *Journal of Neuroimage: Clinical*, 20, pp. 102–109. Available at: https://doi.org/10.1016/j.nicl.2019.102045.

Breton, J. (2020) *The Role of the Prefrontal Cortex in Stress and Motivation* (Doctoral dissertation, UC Berkeley). Available at: https://escholarship.org/uc/item/90t6d53n.

Brodal, P. (2004) *The Central Nervous System: Structure and Function*. New York: Oxford University Press.

Cambridge Dictionary Online (2022) Available at: https://dictionary.cambridge.org/dictionary/english/neuroscience.

Conkbayir, M. (2017) *Early Childhood and Neuroscience: Theory, Research and Implications for Practice*. London: Bloomsbury Publishing.

Diamond, M. and Hopson, J. (1999) *Magic Trees of the Mind: How to Nurture Your Child's Intelligence, Creativity, and Healthy Emotions from Birth Through Adolescence*. New York: Penguin.

Diamond, M. C. (2001) Response of the brain to enrichment. *Anais da Academia Brasileira de Ciências*, 73(2), pp. 210–220. Available at: https://doi.org/10.1590/S0001-37652001000200006.

Dumontheil, I. and Mareschal, D. (2020) An Introduction to Brain and Cognitive Development; The key concepts you need to know. In: M. S. Thomas, D. Mareschal and I. Dumontheil eds. *Educational Neuroscience: Development Across the Life Span*. Abingdon: Routledge, pp. 23–49.

Dunsworth, H. M. and Eccleston, L. (2015) The evolution of difficult childbirth and helpless hominin infants. *Annual Review of Anthropology*, 44(1), pp. 55–69. Available at: https://doi.org/10.1146/annurev-anthro-102214-013918.

Forbes, T. A. and Gallo, V. (2017) All wrapped up: environmental effects on myelination. *Trends in neurosciences*, 40(9), pp. 572–587. Available at: https://doi.org/10.1016/j.tins.2017.06.009.

Ford, J. D., Grasso, D. J., Elhai, J. D. and Courtois, C. A. (2015) *Posttraumatic Stress Disorder: Scientific and Professional Dimensions*. 2nd edn. San Diego: Academic Press.

Fragkaki, I., Stins, J., Roelofs, K., Jongedijk, R. A. and Hagenaars, M. A. (2016) Tonic immobility differentiates stress responses in PTSD. *Journal of Brain and Behavior*, 6(11). Available at: https://doi.org/10.1002/brb3.546.

Garcia-Rill, E. (2019) *Arousal in Neurological and Psychiatric Diseases*. London: Academic Press.

Garvey, D. (2018) *Nurturing Personal, Social and Emotional Development in Early Childhood: A Practical Guide to Understanding Brain Development and Young Children's Behaviour*. London: Jessica Kingsley Publishers.

Goswami, U. (2020) *Cognitive Development and Cognitive Neuroscience: The Learning Brain*. 2nd edn. Abingdon: Routledge.

Hagenaars, M. A., Oitzl, M. and Roelofs, K. (2014) Updating freeze: aligning animal and human research. *Journal of Neuroscience and Biobehavioral Reviews*, 47, pp. 165–176. Available at: https://doi.org/10.1016/j.neubiorev.2014.07.021.

Hagenaars, M. A. (2016) Tonic immobility and PTSD in a large community sample. *Journal of Experimental Psychopathology*, 7(2), pp. 246–260. Available at: https://doi.org/10.5127/Fjep.051915.

Heaney, K. (2017) *When Stress Makes You Fall Asleep*. New York: New York Magazine - The Cut. [blog] 11 July. Available at: https://www.thecut.com/2017/07/when-stress-makes-you-fall-asleep.html.

Heghes, N. E. and Schiopu, C. G. (2019) *The Stockholm Syndrome Psychosocial Varieties and Interdisciplinary Implications*. Research Association for Interdisciplinary Studies. Working Papers 009NH. November 2019. pp. 66–71. Available at: https://ideas.repec.org/p/smo/ipaper/009nh.html.

Mental Health Foundation (2022) *National U.K.-based Charity Aiming to Support People to Understand, Protect and Sustain Mental Health*. Available at: https://www.mentalhealth.org.uk/a-to-z/s/stress.

MIND (2022) *National U.K.-based Charity Aiming to Raise Awareness and Understanding, and Campaign and Provide Advice in Relation to Mental Health*. Available at: https://www.mind.org.uk/information-support/types-of-mental-health-problems/stress/what-is-stress/.

Nordqvist, C. (2016) *What is Neuroscience?* Brighton: Medical News Today. Available at: www.medicalnewstoday.com/articles/248680.php.

Paredes, M. F., James, D., Gil-Perotin, S., Kim, H. Cotter, J. A., Ng, C., Sandoval, K., Rowitch, D. H., Xu, D., McQuillen, P. S. and Garcia-Verdugo, J. M. (2016) Extensive migration of young neurons into the infant human frontal lobe. *Science* 354(6308). Available at: https://doi.org/10.1126/science.aaf7073.

Roelofs, K. (2017) Freeze For Action: Neurobiological mechanisms in animal and human freezing. *Philosophical Transactions of The Royal Society, London. Series B, Biological Sciences*, 372(1718), p. 20160206. Available at: https://doi.org/10.1098/rstb.2016.0206.

Rosenberg, K. and Trevathan, W. R. (2002) Birth, obstetrics, and human evolution. *BJOG: International Journal of Obstetrics and Gynaecology*, 109(11), pp. 1199–1206. Available at: https://doi.org/10.1046/j.1471-0528.2002.00010.x.

Schultz, A. (1949) Sex differences in the pelves of primates. *American Journal of Physical Anthropology*, 7(3), pp. 401–424. Available at: https://doi.org/10.1002/ajpa.1330070307.

Shonkoff, J. P. and Phillips, D. A., eds. (2000) *From Neurons to Neighborhoods: The Science of Early Childhood Development.* Washington, DC: National Academy Press.

Stynoski, J. L., Torres-Mendoza, Y., Sasa-Marin, M. and Saporito, R. A. (2014) Evidence of maternal provisioning of alkaloid-based chemical defenses in the Strawberry Poison Frog Oophaga Pumilio. *Journal of Ecology*, 95(3), pp. 587–593. Available at: https://doi.org /10.1890/13-0927.1.

University of Queensland, Australia: Queensland Brain Institute. (2022) *The Brain.* Available at: https://qbi.uq.edu.au/brain/brain-anatomy/ central-nervous-system-brain-and-spinal-cord.

Wells, J. C. K., Desilva, J. M. and Stock, J. T. (2012) The obstetric dilemma: an ancient game of Russian roulette, or a variable dilemma sensitive to ecology? *Yearbook of Physical Anthropology*, 149(55), pp. 40–71. Available at: https://doi.org/10.1002/ajpa .22160.

Yong, S. J. (2021) Persistent brainstem dysfunction in Long-COVID: a hypothesis. *Journal of ACS Chemical Neuroscience*, 12(4), pp. 573–580. Available at: https://doi.org/10.1021/acschemneuro .0c00793.

Web Resources

These resources are useful across the book, but rather than repeat them in every bibliography they are here for convenience. Most do not have dates as they are regularly updated. The text in bold is for ease of reference/searching.

Alberta Family Wellness Initiative. *Serve and Return.* Available at: https://www.albertafamilywellness.org/what-we-know/serve-and -return#:~:text=Serve%20and%20return%20works%20like,a %20toy%20or%20a%20laugh

Brain Builders *[video]*

Get an introduction to the Brain Story in this accessible and engaging video. The AFWI developed the video with considerable input from our partners at the Harvard Center on the Developing Child and the FrameWorks Institute.
Available at: https://www.albertafamilywellness.org/resources/video/how-brains-are-built-core-story-of-brain-development

Brains: Journey to Resilience *[video]*

Discover the science of resilience in this engaging and information-packed video. In a world where human brains inch across snowy landscapes, where perils lurk in every shadow, one community will rally behind a struggling brain – and just might change the world in the process. Learn about the resilience scale in this scientifically rigorous (and cinematically epic) resource created by the AFWI in consultation with the FrameWorks Institute and the Harvard Center on the Developing Child at Harvard University.
Available at: https://www.albertafamilywellness.org/resources/video/brains-journey-to-resilience

Oxford Brain Story: Brain Story Certification *[Training Programme – Free]*

The University of Oxford, in partnership with the Alberta Family Wellness Initiative, is working to share knowledge about the science of brain development for families and professionals. This is important information for everybody to understand how our earliest experiences can affect our long-term mental and physical health.
This free online course is for professionals seeking a deeper understanding of brain development and its consequences for resilience and lifelong health.

Videos of more than 30 leading experts in neurobiology and mental health
Certification in Brain Story science
19 modules (self-paced)

Available at: https://www.oxfordbrainstory.org/for-professionals
or
https://www.albertafamilywellness.org/training/

Center on the Developing Child at Harvard University

Main Website: Available at: https://developingchild.harvard.edu/
Brain Architecture. Available at: https://developingchild.harvard.edu/science/key-concepts/brain-architecture/
Key Concepts. Available at: https://developingchild.harvard.edu/science/key-concepts/
Resilience. Available at: https://developingchild.harvard.edu/science/key-concepts/resilience/
Self-Regulation and Executive Function. Available at: https://developingchild.harvard.edu/science/key-concepts/executive-function/
Serve and Return. Available at: https://developingchild.harvard.edu/science/key-concepts/serve-and-return/
Serve and Return. Available at: https://developingchild.harvard.edu/resources/building-babies-brains-through-play-mini-parenting-master-class/
Toxic Stress. Available at: https://developingchild.harvard.edu/science/key-concepts/toxic-stress/

Center on the Developing Child. *Connecting the Brain to the Rest of the Body: Early Childhood Development and Lifelong Health Are Deeply Intertwined.* [video] Available at: https://developingchild.harvard.edu/resources/connecting-the-brain-to-the-rest-of-the-body-early-childhood-development-and-lifelong-health-are-deeply-intertwined/

Center on the Developing Child (2022). *How Racism Can Affect Child Development*. Available at: https://developingchild.harvard.edu/resources/racism-and-ecd/

National Scientific Council on the Developing Child (2020). *Connecting the Brain to the Rest of the Body: Early Childhood Development and Lifelong Health Are Deeply Intertwined Working Paper No. 15*. Available at: https://developingchild.harvard.edu/resources/inbrief-connecting-the-brain-to-the-rest-of-the-body/

CourseHero. *Introduction to Psychology*.

OpenStax College is a non-profit organization committed to improving student access to quality learning materials. Our free textbooks go through a rigorous editorial publishing process. Our texts are developed and peer-reviewed by educators to ensure they are readable, accurate, and meet the scope and sequence requirements of today's college courses.

Available at: https://www.coursehero.com/study-guides/wsu-sandbox/introduction-16/

Covid-19: Mental Health in the Pandemic:

British Medical Journal: Available at: https://www.bmj.com/coronavirus (Search 'Mental Health' - All articles open access)

Childcare Research: Available at: https://childcare-during-covid.org/

Mental Health Foundation: Available at: https://www.mentalhealth.org.uk/our-work/research/coronavirus-mental-health-pandemic

Early Education (2021). *Birth to 5 Matters: Non-statutory Guidance for the Early Years Foundation Stage*. St. Albans: Early Education (on behalf of Early Years Coalition).

Overview of topics. Available at: https://birthto5matters.org.uk/

Additional resource list. Available at: https://birthto5matters.org.uk/resources/

King's College London: School of Neuroscience: Institute of Psychiatry, Psychology and Neuroscience. *What Is Neuroscience?* Available at: https://www.kcl.ac.uk/Neuroscience/About/What-Is-Neuroscience

OECD (Organisation for Economic Co-operation and Development) (2002). *Understanding the Brain: Towards a New Learning Science.* Paris: OECD Publishing. Available at: https://www.oecd-ilibrary .org/education/understanding-the-brain_9789264174986-en#:~:text =This%20book%20examines%20how%20new,teaching%20and %20developing%20educational%20policies.

PACEY (Professional Association for Childcare and Early Years) (2016). *Theories of Child Development: A practice guide to help you understand theories of child development and their influence on early years practice.* Bromley: PACEY. Available at: https://www.pacey .org.uk/Pacey/media/Website-files/PACEY%20member%20practice %20guides%20(PDFs)/PG28-Theories-of-child-development.pdf

As we have considered, right from birth, the brains of young children need to work extra hard, from the newborn babies whose neurons need to travel huge distances to end up in the correct places, to young children where the messages may take longer to travel to the correct part of the body. Let's continue our journey looking at how we can use this, and other neuroscientific information, to inform our understanding of early childhood.

If this is a journey of exploration, then maybe we can emulate those great explorers such as Sir David Attenborough – what would Sir David do, or say? Maybe something along the lines of 'here is the lesser-spotted small fry in its natural habitat'. Maybe that gives us a clue. Perhaps the easiest way to consider this is to look at this from an anthropology angle – to study human development, culture, and environments. Where do we find children, where do children 'exist' and what is their natural habitat? In other words, let us study environments.

In terms of humans, there are two very distinct, but integrated environments – the physical and the emotional. Just like the animal species studied by the great explorers, the human species has some environments where we can thrive – and others, well, not so much. In terms of physical environments, if you think about where humans live across the globe, we exist in extremes of conditions, temperatures, or availability of resources, for example. Likewise, in terms of emotional environments, we have extremes of safety and extremes of wellbeing. All of which co-exist on this sometimes-topsy-turvy planet we call home.

For humans (children and adults), our experience of our environments starts with being the centre of our own world. This is what Bronfenbrenner (1977, 1979, 1992) termed the 'microsystem'. The microsystem is defined as the immediate surroundings, and how they are experienced by the person

DOI: 10.4324/9781003154846-2

at the centre (whether child or adult). Home, family, childcare, school, and friendships, for example, are all versions of a microsystem (and we'll explore the other systems in a later chapter).

Throughout life, relationships are key to human development. Whether for a child, or an adult, in terms of the microsystem, we are each at the centre of our own worlds. The people in our immediate circle, the roles they have, the things we do together – and importantly how those things are experienced by the person at the centre – all influence how we grow and develop, or sadly do not, as the case may be. In other words, our physical environments, but also how all of these things make us feel – our emotional environments – are both of great importance.

In terms of neuroscience, there are some strong clues as to what helps. Professor Usha Goswami is Professor of Cognitive Developmental Neuroscience at the University of Cambridge, and offers the following:

> The easiest and most effective way to support a child's development is by providing the best possible learning [development] environments as consistently as possible in all aspects of their life – in the home and family, at nursery [or setting], at school, and in our wider culture and society.
>
> (Goswami, 2020: xix)

This is particularly helpful for those of us interested in early childhood. Here we have some very, very strong indications of the importance of adults in children's lives – after all, it is adults that provide, create and maintain both the physical and emotional environments within which babies and children grow, learn, develop, and flourish (or not, as the case may be).

REFLECTIVE PRACTICE

Considering Physical and Emotional Environments

Re-read the quote from Professor Usha Goswami (2020: xix). There are some key words in the quote:

Best possible: which means greatest imaginable, finest conceivable, ultimately feasible and so on.

Consistently: which means regularly, reliably, steadily, constantly, repeatedly, dependably and so on.

And finally, '**all aspects**', which is highlighted as encompassing all areas of a child's life.

(Part 1):

Now, consider the following questions:

(You might want to jot down a few thoughts as you'll need them for Part 2.)

What do you think of when thinking about these words/phrases? Are there particular children/families/circumstances you think about?

Why do you think that is?

How does this link to your practice/experience?

What is working well?

What might need further consideration?

Who might you need to speak to?

Where might you look for further information/support?

Any other thoughts or reflections?

(Part 2):

Now, let's put that into context – for each question in Part 1:

What are the elements of the physical environment(s) you were considering for each question?

What are the elements of the emotional environment(s) you were considering for each question?

Your reflections should clearly show why the physical and emotional environments are both of importance and need finely balancing. In addition, it should be fairly clear as to where things are going particularly well, and also where further thought is needed. This should help with a starting point for reflection and thinking about any developments needed, as well as future planning or practice.

The Science of Environments

From as early as the 1700s, the child development theorists Jean-Jacques Rousseau, Friedrich Froebel, Jean Piaget, Lev Vygotsky, Maria Montessori, John Bowlby, Urie Bronfenbrenner, and many, many others all explored the relationships children have with their physical and emotional environments. These giants of childhood development research and theory all considered how we, as humans, develop (or not) depending on our environments and experiences.

Much of the child development knowledge we now understand was based on their observations, painstakingly recorded, mainly by hand, and in minute detail. The theorists observed children in their physical environment, covering every angle, aspect, and element. In addition, some theorists started to explore the emotional environments children find themselves in and considered the impacts adults have on children. For example, Maria Montessori used her observations of children and adult interactions to study the impact of adults' behaviours on children. This then led to her very specific expectations of the staff in the Casa dei Bambini schools in Italy:

> The teacher's task is first to nourish and assist, to watch, encourage, guide, induce, rather than to interfere, prescribe, or restrict.
>
> (Montessori, 1912: xxi)

As each theorist developed their ideas, reports and articles followed, books were written and published, and the ideas cascaded. Ideas were developed, strengthened, and reinforced – or disputed, discredited, or debunked. Many were, and continue to be, debated.

Fast forward to the 21st century, and now we have the science and technology to explore childhood in a way never before possible. It still amazes me that we can use our technology to look inside babies' brains. The science around neuroimaging is quite fascinating. Many of you will have had x-rays or ultrasound scans in the radiology departments of the hospital and seen the pictures of the inside of your body. You might have even had an electroencephalogram (EEG), which looks at electrical activity in the brain.

The Magnetic Resonance Imaging (MRI) tube-like machine, which scans an entire body, is probably also familiar, if not personally, then at least through images on the TV. Similarly, we have functional Magnetic Resonance Imaging (fMRI) that can measure the tiny changes in blood flow which can be linked to what our brain is doing at that exact time. Meanwhile, Near Infrared Spectroscopy (NIRS) uses blood and oxygen to measure brain activity. And whilst Positron Emission Tomography (PET) sounds like something from Star Trek, this amazing technology means we can actually see images of neurons firing within the brain.

What many of these methods allow us to do, is take detailed images at a particular time and compare the outcomes. This, of course, is where the importance of environments comes in. In simple terms this could be taking an image of the brain of a baby who is distressed, and comparing that to the images a few seconds later of the baby being comforted by a caring adult.... And importantly, we can see biological evidence of how the brain reacts to different situations (Van Puyvelde et al., 2021). In addition, we can also use this technology to look at the size and structure of the brain, and see changes over time:

> After birth ... brain development consists mainly of the growth of connections between neurons: *synaptogenesis* [which] leads the infant brain to double in size during the first year of life.
>
> (Goswami, 2020: xix, *emphasis in original*)

Goswami, and other colleagues, only know this because of the ever-expanding technology at our fingertips – technology that Rousseau, Froebel, Montessori, et al., could only have dreamed about.

This new learning then helps with our understanding of biology, neuro-biology and so on, and how this links to the importance of early childhood. However, with new learning and understanding comes debate. The trouble with new learning is that it is just that – new. This means that different areas of science, education, and other fields of study can often have opposing views as they each make new discoveries. It also means that new discoveries can be misused or misinterpreted, whether unintentionally or indeed purposefully, to 'prove' a particular point. In terms of neuroscience, these are often called 'neuromyths' (Organisation for Economic Co-operation and Development, 2002). An example would be that early childhood is often described as a 'criti-cal period'. This can imply that early childhood is the *only* time for learning a specific skill, for example. Of course, this is not true, and there are some things that some children learn and can do, which other people do not learn or cannot do until much later (riding a bike would be a good example here). Therefore, the term 'sensitive period' is preferred (at least for the moment any-way). This covers the idea that this period is the most sensitive (or responsive), but not critical or indeed the *only* time for learning and development.

In terms of early childhood, the debates and misinterpretations are very real. One example of this is the famous image of the two brains origi-nally from the Perry (2002) study. The images are repeatedly used for a whole host of claims on the importance of the earliest years. In actual fact, the images show a healthy brain, and a brain that has experienced *extreme* neglect and trauma – a brain almost completely deprived of an emotional environment, and with a very, very, very limited physical environment. I am sure you have seen the image, but often the accompanying text and reference to the original study is missing. The two images clearly show the importance of the physical and emotional environments to the growing brain. Unfortunately, the image has been misused so many times that Dr Perry has asked that it is no longer used (@BDPerry Twitter 17/07/2019).

Sadly, examples such as this means that the science from other areas can then also be called into question. This is particularly true of child devel-opment in relation to early adversity and the impacts of poor physical and emotional environments. This can cause extreme confusion for those of us trying to champion quality early childhood practice. The danger is that the debates take over from the central role of the environments – both physical and emotional. And… the roles we as adults have to play.

In effect, we end up going round in circles debating the 'strength' of the importance of the earliest years. This then distracts from the facts we do know: human brains are born incomplete, they grow the most in the earliest years, and they rely on adults to help them grow. And… that often, it is the simplest of things that make the biggest difference.

Regardless of debates, all the research seems to agree on one thing – early childhood is important:

> A fundamental paradox exists and is unavoidable: development in the early years is both highly robust and highly vulnerable. Although there have been long-standing debates about how much the early years really matter in the larger scheme of lifelong development, our conclusion is unequivocal:
>
> What happens during the first months and years of life matters a lot, not because this period of development provides an indelible blueprint for adult well-being, but because it sets either a sturdy or fragile stage for what follows.
>
> (Shonkoff and Phillips, 2000: 5)

In other words, the earliest years are vitally important, but as Shonkoff and Phillips (2000: 5) point out, this is not about an 'indelible blueprint'. This is not saying that all children 'must' have some implausibly 'perfect' childhood. Nor is it saying that children who sadly experience early adversity, difficulties, abuse and/or trauma will be 'irreparably damaged'. (Note: This is not a book about safeguarding and child protection – there are plenty of useful, relevant sources of information about that elsewhere, which I urge you to explore at your own pace.)

The neuroscientific evidence now clearly shows that what happens in the earliest years may make a strong foundation – or a foundation that is a little more difficult, complicated, or tricky and therefore may need more support. Therefore, I would like us to concentrate on what brains need to develop, and what we (as adults) can do to support this – and in terms of this chapter, the environments we provide.

Environments – Physical and Emotional

For the purpose of this book, we will use the following terms:

Physical environment – to mean buildings, furniture, indoors and outdoors.
Emotional environment – to mean, how places (or people) make us (and children) feel.

To investigate this in more detail, let's go on a little journey exploring how we, as adults, feel in some environments. First off, let's consider the physical and emotional elements of an environment. This reflective practice exercise is about exploring how some places make us feel, and considering why that might be. The reflection is in two parts, but for both parts it would be useful to think about the same environment.

Think about an environment that has made an impression on you. It could be for work purposes, personal purposes or perhaps a social visit somewhere. In your 'mind's eye' really explore the place – how did it look, how did it feel, what did you notice, who else was there, etc. You might want to jot down a few notes as you go.

REFLECTIVE PRACTICE
Exploring Environments (Part 1)

Physical Environment

Let's concentrate on the physical environment to start with. When you think about the physical environment:

What images do you think of?
What kind of building was it?
What about your senses: noises and smells, etc.?
    Was it too hot/too cold, too dark/bright, etc.?
Was anyone else there?
What thoughts spring to mind about this place?

Exploring Environments (Part 2)

Emotional Environment

Now, think about the emotional environment. What springs to mind?

How did you feel when you went to this place?
How did the building make you feel?
How did the people make you feel?

And for all of these questions:
Why do you think that is?

The chances are we can all probably remember extremes of the spectrum – those places where we felt comfortable, safe, and cared for, and those where we did not. Also, it is highly likely that in the places where we did feel comfortable, safe, and cared for it is because of the people. If you'll bear with me I'll use a personal example for a moment to explore this. I have written elsewhere about the sadness my husband and I experienced of not being able to have our own children. What I have not discussed in much detail is the journey that experience took us on.

Countless appointments, in numerous buildings with endless corridors. Many of the appointments involved intrusive, painful, and worrying tests. Many of them involved tears and sadness. All of them involved people. Over 10 years of finding our way around new buildings and meeting new people.

Some of the buildings were old, some state of the art new. Some were bright and airy, some were dark and hot. But... and it's a big but... the buildings did not matter – the people did...

Throughout all of it (and it is over 25 years ago now), I can still remember the people. I can remember the ones who made us feel comfortable, safe, and cared for – and the ones who did not. I can remember the ones who listened and heard – and the ones who did not. I can remember the ones who offered comfort – and the ones who did not.

Please do not be upset by this story or feel sad for us. All of this was a long time ago, and we've had a long time to come to terms with it. We have numerous children, godchildren, and nephews and nieces in our lives who bring us great joy, and we have done many things that might not have been so easy had our lives taken a different path. The reason for using this personal journey is I believe it shows so starkly the importance of the people – and how long those memories stay with us.

I am sure you have similar stories where you have had to do something quite difficult and the people who were around you helped – or did not, as the case may be. If we bring this back to our world of early childhood, I am sure you can see where this is going.

If we imagine two environments:

Environment 1:

The building is bright and modern. The furniture and accessories (resources) are pristine and beautifully displayed.
The people are uninterested, lack warmth and understanding and spend most of the time talking to each other.

Environment 2:

The building is quite old and needs some repairs. The heating doesn't always work. The furniture and accessories (resources) are clean, and clearly much loved.
The people are warm and friendly, enthusiastic about their jobs and keen to help. They listen to everyone and get involved wherever they can. The atmosphere is one of thoughtfulness, kindness, and respect.

Whether we are talking environments we find ourselves in as adults, children's own home environments or professional childhood environments, I am sure we can all think of many examples of both environment 1 *and* environment 2, and probably combinations of them both. My question would be – which environment would you feel comfortable in? (And which environment do you think children would feel comfortable in?) And importantly – why do you think that?

I am not saying that it is acceptable for children (or adults) to be in cold, damp environments. It is more nuanced than that, and a range of factors will of course impact on how we, or indeed children, feel. But I am sure you can see the points being made here:

> What is in a space, a room or a yard, and how it is arranged can affect the behaviour of people; it can make it easier to act in certain kinds of ways, harder to act in others. … The whole setting gives us cues about expected behaviour, and generally we do what we have been invited to do … in a similar way, particular settings invite children to involve themselves in particular activities, and the extent of children's constructive participation in the activity will depend in large part on how well … the surrounding physical space meet their "hunger, attitudes and interests."
>
> (Kritchevsky et al., 1977: 5)

In other words, 'how well' the *people* have thought about what the 'space' looks and feels like. As Lella Gandini (author of *The Hundred Languages of Children: The Reggio Emilia Approach to Early Childhood Education*) comments:

> The environment is the most visible aspect of the work… It conveys the message that this is a place where adults have thought about the quality and instructive power of space. The layout of the physical space is welcoming and fosters encounters, communication and relationships. The arrangement of structures, objects, and activities encourages choices, problem solving, and discoveries in the process of learning. There is attention to detail everywhere.
>
> (cited in Curtis and Carter, 2003: 13)

If we look back through these two quotes, the thing that strikes me is the number of emotion-inducing/emotion-related words and phrases they both contain:

Behaviour	Interests	How well
Easier	Thought	Relationships
Harder	Power	Encourages
Expected	Welcoming	Invited
Process	Fosters	Involve
Learning	Encounters	Problem solving
Attention to detail	Communication	Discoveries
Attitudes	Participation	Choices

To me this demonstrates the importance of the emotional environment within the physical environment – and crucially that it is us, as adults, that create that environment.

The Role of the Adult

In relation to the early childhood environment, the role of the adult is pivotal. We decide what goes into the environment and what does not. We decide where children go, what they do, when they do it, and how they do it. And… generally, it is our behaviours, actions and deeds that steer how the environment feels emotionally. I do not want to go into the role of the adult in too much detail here, as we explore this more in a later chapter. What I do want to consider is how we, as adults, and the environments we provide, impact on the neurobiology of children.

As we mentioned in Chapter 1, the sympathetic and parasympathetic nervous systems play a key role in how we feel when we are worried, scared, or frightened. There is also a key link here to how various environments make us feel. If we think back to the reflective exercise 'Exploring Environments', we will probably be able to pinpoint the environments where the parasympathetic nervous system came into play. For example, considering the environment that had us feeling stressed and anxious, and how it is not until we leave that we let out that huge breath we had been unconscious of holding in. It is afterwards that we feel our heartrate reduce and breathing return to normal. It can almost feel as if a fog lifts from our brains and we can concentrate and think again… Or we will be able to remember being inside the difficult environment and the people who helped our parasympathetic systems return to normal – the people who really listened, and who helped us to feel comfortable, safe, and cared for.

In terms of early childhood settings, one of the key elements to this is the importance of what is termed 'continuous provision'. Leroy, a practitioner in an inner city preschool, offers the following reflections on continuous provision.

Continuous Provision: Comforting and Challenging

In our setting, we try to use open-ended and traditional resources, photographs, displays, and books as part of continuous provision both indoors and outdoors. We know some of our children have quite difficult home lives, so continuous provision is vitally important. They need to know that when they come in, they can play with the things that they know and love. The continuity helps children to feel safe and secure, in comfortable surroundings in which they are familiar – and children who feel safe are more likely to be able to learn. Also, once the children are in the building, and parents have left, we have open access to the outdoor area, as we know this is important for some children. This is especially true for some boys who often learn better outdoors, and for some children who we know live in flats.

Indoors, we have areas that cover the usual things such as sand, water, playdough, home corner, books, creativity and small world, etc. Outdoors, we have space for physical play (balls, bikes, tubes and crates, etc.), den building, exploration resources, larger water and sand play and space to be quieter. We also have woodwork, but that is always supported by an adult. Continuous provision allows children to revisit and expand on their ideas and learning. In the creative area, for example, we try to leave children's artwork and models so children can return to them if they wish. We model how to use real tools, such as staplers, scissors, and tape dispensers, and as children become more confident with the environment we introduce more complex ideas, such as powder paint for mixing. We try not to change these areas too often, but when we do, we get the children to help, and we listen carefully to their ideas. However, we do add in enhancements to respond to a child's interest or to encourage exploration or language. This might be putting farm animals in the sand if a child has been on a visit to a farm, or putting cultural decorations in the home corner for children to explore at different festival times, for example.

The one area of provision where we try to ensure consistent continuity is the home corner. Yes, we add in enhancements/different resources, or change things that are damaged, but we try not to change the overall structure. Although some of our families live in very difficult circumstances, and some live in very different homes, most families have similar routines and structures. Children find comfort in repeating those familiar things from home, such as cooking, bathing baby or cleaning. We can have up to 10 different languages, but we see children using the space to build relationships with other children as they recognise and join in with familiar routines, even if they do not speak the same language. As adults, we see glimpses of home which tell us very clearly what is happening in the child's life. Sometimes, these 'role play' observations can cause safeguarding concerns and we act on those. Sometimes though, they cause a smile too, I remember one child clearly showing their understanding of a difficult telephone conversation – the air was blue as she slammed the phone down!

Our provision aims to celebrate and support children's understanding of our world. We have families from a range of backgrounds, including traveller families, foster families, and children with same sex parents. We try to ensure our resources are diverse and inclusive, so small world play always has diverse figures, and more than one mummy and daddy, for example. We are careful with the language we use too – and always ask parents how to pronounce names correctly and how they want to be referred to.

In our setting, we believe continuous provision should support all areas of learning and development. When new children start, practitioners support the newer children to understand how the areas work, and talk about the resources and the things the children are doing. As children become more confident, we support them to extend their play, challenge themselves, take risks, and try out, test and develop their own ideas. Over time, we can withdraw, and the children can then explore freely and learn from the environment.

One of the reasons continuous provision is so important in early childhood, is that consistency helps humans to feel safe. We like our meals at roughly the same time, our homes ordered in a particular manner, and our relationships to behave in certain ways – it is the same for children. Consistency does not mean regimented, and I am not saying children should have every minute of the day scheduled to within an inch. But, generally speaking, chaos and uncertainty, and being unsure of what might or could happen, worries the majority of people and that includes children. One of the key findings from research around the world on the impact on mental health during the Covid-19 pandemic, was that people of all ages, including children, found the uncertainty the most worrying aspect (Gloster et al., 2020; Nitschke et al., 2021; Rettie and Daniels, 2020; Zhou and Li, 2020).

Furthermore, continuous provision is important because it provides a feeling of safety. If we think back to Chapter 1 and the discussions around fight, flight, fear and so on, a place where we feel safe means we do not have to worry about potential threats (real or imaginary). Imagine being a small child – if you know the layout of a room, for example, then there is less need to worry about what 'might' be lurking around a corner.

Feeling safe is part of our neurobiology (meaning in relation to the nervous system) and as we mentioned in Chapter 1:

The sympathetic system helps in preparing for stress/stressful situations. The parasympathetic system brings everything back to normal afterwards.

This is important to know when we are thinking about the significance of continuous provision.

REFLECTIVE PRACTICE

Importance of Continuous Provision

Kaatib is 18 months old, and lives with his mum and dad, and older sister Alyssa, who is 4. Kaatib wakes at 5.30am. It has been a difficult night for all the family as the neighbour's car alarm went off half a dozen times.

At breakfast time it is suddenly apparent that someone forgot to buy milk – this results in a short, but vocal disagreement between the grownups.

Kaatib and Alyssa both want the red cup for their drink.

On to getting washed and dressed, Kaatib refuses to use the toothpaste and Alyssa can only find one shoe.

Getting ready to leave and the zip on Kaatib's coat gets stuck – it takes at least 5 minutes to un-stick it. The car is also having a difficult morning and takes a while to start.

Finally, on the way, the traffic is awful and every traffic light on the journey seems to be at red. Alyssa is singing songs at the top of her voice and Kaatib is shouting and pointing at every other car, bus, truck, and lorry.

Now consider the following questions:

How do you think this kind of morning would make you feel, as an adult?

Why do you think that?

How do you think this kind of morning would make Kaatib/Alyssa feel?

Why do you think that?

Now imagine getting to your destination and nothing looks like it did when you left. Imagine someone has moved all the furniture around. Your favourite items are not where you thought they would be. You cannot find *anything*.

How do you think you might feel, as an adult?
Why do you think that?
How do you think a child might feel?
Why do you think that?

For many people (and children) this is a fairly normal morning. However, the likelihood is that we would still be feeling stressed, anxious, and frazzled before we had even arrived at our destination. In biological terms, our sympathetic nervous system is now on 'high alert' after the stressful morning. This means that our breathing, heartrate, and hormone levels (such as adrenaline and cortisol), for example, are all faster/higher than normal, even if we are not fully aware of them. To then arrive at a building that suddenly feels unfamiliar could cause further worry, panic, and stress.

In turn, this then means that our parasympathetic system cannot bring everything back to normal because the destination is no longer the familiar, safe, secure space that it previously was. I know this can all sound a little far-fetched – why would a simple thing like moving furniture, for example, cause us to feel unsafe?

Let's look at this in a slightly different way:

Having a morning full of a series of seemingly small, but nevertheless stressful events puts the sympathetic system 'on alert'. *Biologically*, our breathing, heartrate, hormone levels, etc., are all 'heightened'. Our bodies then struggle to produce hormones that help us to feel safe (such as oxytocin, dopamine, and serotonin).

Arriving at a familiar space helps us to feel safe and helps our parasympathetic nervous system return our breathing, heartrate, and hormones, etc., to normal.
This then means we can think and concentrate more clearly.

OR,

Further small stressful events occur, and our stress system stays in 'alert mode'.
Additional stressful events (even seemingly small ones), such as an unfamiliar environment, means our stress-alert levels rise, and feelings of being unsafe are intensified.
Our hormone levels rise further. The parasympathetic nervous system cannot do its job and return systems to normal. This is biological.
Regulating our feelings and emotions is difficult, which in turn will influence our reactions and behaviours.
We cannot think or concentrate on anything except what it is that we are worried, anxious, or stressed about.

Therefore, in very simplified terms:

Stress systems stay in high alert when we do not feel safe.
Familiar environments help us to feel safe.

And therefore,

Continuous provision helps children to feel safe.
Feeling safe means human systems can return to normal levels.
We can then also regulate feelings and emotions.
This means we can think and concentrate.

... and be more likely to be able to listen, understand and be present with what is happening around us – whether we are children or adults.

REFLECTIVE PRACTICE

Exploring Environments

Consider the environments (both physical and emotional) you provide for children.

Why are the environments offered in a particular way?
What influenced them?
Do they meet all children's needs? How do you know?
Are they underpinned by research, reflection and evaluation based on observations?
Do children like them?
How do you know?
Do children feel safe?
How do you know?
Do children have opportunities to influence/shape the environment?
When? How? Why?
And... if not, why not?
Now, thinking about this chapter, are there elements of the environments that you think need further thought, reflection, or consideration?

What might you need to do?
Who might you need to speak to?
Where could you look for ideas/support, etc.?
Anything else?

Reflecting on environments in this way, it becomes easy to realise why supporters of the Reggio Emilia approach advocate for understanding of "the environment as the third teacher" (Gandini, 1998: 177). It also becomes easy to see the importance of understanding how the emotional environment and physical environment are inextricably entwined, and how, at times, we all need a 'supportive' someone who helps us.

It should be clear from the discussions here, and your reflections throughout this chapter, why the environments, both physical and emotional, are equally important. The environments influence how we feel, react, and behave. This in turn influences our ability to think, concentrate and be present with what is happening around us. Neuroscience can now prove how, from birth, the environments around us are of vital importance to the human brain, and our very biology.

The neuroscience umbrella is vast. The sciences behind the technology, biology, and neurobiology we have discussed in this chapter are helping us to understand the impact of physical and emotional environments on the development of children's brains. In addition, there are what is known as the behavioural sciences. These include psychology, cognitive psychology, educational neuroscience and so on. These link closely to what we have touched on briefly here – in terms of behaviours, actions, attitudes, and self-regulation – and we will explore more of this in the next chapter.

Chapter Reflection

Thinking back over this chapter, consider the various elements (sections, quotes, reflective exercises, terminology, etc.). Are there any elements that:

Were particularly useful?
Need re-reading, or more thought or reflection?
You want to look up and/or explore further?

Any other thoughts or reflections?

Bibliography

The following are books, articles, web pages, organisations, documents, etc. that I have found useful (online versions, all accessed 20 July 2022). Some are directly referenced in this chapter – some are included as valuable sources of background reading that might be helpful. See also web resources at the end of Chapter 1.

Brodal, P. (2004) *The Central Nervous System: Structure and Function.* Oxford: Oxford University Press.

Bronfenbrenner, U. (1977) Toward an experimental ecology of human development. *American Psychologist,* 32, pp. 513–531. Available at: https://psycnet.apa.org/doi/10.1037/0003-066X.32.7.513.

Bronfenbrenner, U. (1979) *The Ecology of Human Development: Experiments by Nature and Design.* Cambridge, MA: Harvard University Press.

Bronfenbrenner, U. (1986) Ecology of the family as a context for human development. *Developmental Psychology,* 22(6), pp. 723–742. Available at: https://psycnet.apa.org/doi/10.1037/0012-1649.22.6.723.

Bronfenbrenner, U. (1992) *Ecological Systems Theory.* London: Jessica Kingsley Publishers.

Bronfenbrenner, U. and Ceci, S. J. (1994) Nature-nurture reconceptualized in developmental perspective: a bioecological model. *Psychological Review,* 101, pp. 568–586. Available at: https://doi.org/10.1037/0033-295x.101.4.568.

Curtis, D. and Carter, M. (2003) Laying a foundation for living and learning. In: D. Curtis and M. Carter, eds. *Designs for Living and Learning: Transforming Early Childhood Environments.* St. Paul, MN: Redleaf Press, pp. 11–19.

Darragh, J. C. (2006) *The Environment as the Third Teacher. Online Submission.* [ED493517] Available at: https://eric.ed.gov/?id=ED493517.

Edwards, C., Gandini, L. and Forman, G., eds. (2011) *The Hundred Languages of Children: The Reggio Emilia Experience in Transformation.* Santa Barbara, CA: ABC-CLIO.

Gandini, L. (1998) Educational and caring spaces. In: C. Edwards, L. Gandini and G. Forman, eds. *The Hundred Languages of Children: The Reggio Emilia Approach—Advanced Reflections*. 2nd edn. Greenwich, CT: Ablex Publishing Corp, pp. 161–178.

Garvey, D. (2018) *Nurturing Personal, Social and Emotional Development in Early Childhood: A Practical Guide to Understanding Brain Development and Young Children's Behaviour*. London: Jessica Kingsley Publishers.

Gloster, A. T., Lamnisos, D., Lubenko, J., Presti, G., Squatrito, V., Constantinou, M., Nicolaou, C., Papacostas, S., Aydın, G., Chong, Y. Y. and Chien, W. T. (2020) Impact of COVID-19 pandemic on mental health: an international study. *PloS one*, 15(12), p. e0244809. Available at: https://doi.org/10.1371/journal.pone.0244809.

Goswami, U. (2020) *Cognitive Development and Cognitive Neuroscience: The Learning Brain*. 2nd edn. Abingdon: Routledge.

Kritchevsky, S. and Prescott, E. with Walling, L. (1977) *Planning Environments for Young Children: Physical Space*. 2nd edn. Washington, DC: National Association for the Education of Young Children.

Montessori, M. (1912) *The Montessori Method: Scientific Pedagogy as Applied to Child Education in 'The Children's Houses' with Additions and Revisions by the Author* (A. E. George, Trans.). Cambridge, MA: Robert Bentley.

Mooney, C. G. (2013) *Theories of Childhood: An Introduction to Dewey, Montessori, Erikson, Piaget and Vygotsky*. St. Paul, MN: Redleaf Press.

Nitschke, J. P., Forbes, P. A., Ali, N., Cutler, J., Apps, M. A., Lockwood, P. L. and Lamm, C. (2021) Resilience during uncertainty? Greater social connectedness during COVID-19 lockdown is associated with reduced distress and fatigue. *British Journal of Health Psychology*, 26(2), pp. 553–569. Available at: https://doi.org/10 .1111/bjhp.12485.

Perry, B. D. (2002) Childhood experience and the expression of genetic potential: what childhood neglect tells us about nature and nurture. *Brain and Mind*, 3, pp. 79–100. Available at: https://doi.org /10.1023/A:1016557824657.

Rettie, H. and Daniels, J. (2020) Coping and tolerance of uncertainty: predictors and mediators of mental health during the COVID-19 pandemic. *American Psychologist*. Advance online publication. Available at: https://doi.org/10.1037/amp0000710.

Shonkoff, J. P. and Phillips, D. A., eds. (2000) *From Neurons to Neighborhoods: The Science of Early Childhood Development*. Washington, DC: National Academy Press.

Strong-Wilson, T. and Ellis, J. (2007) Children and Place: Reggio Emilia's environment as third teacher. *Theory into Practice*, 46(1), pp. 40–47. Available at: https://doi.org/10.1080/00405840709336547.

Tarr, P. (2004) Consider the walls. *Young Children*, 59(3), pp. 88–92. Available at: http://ocw.umb.edu/early-education-development/ echd-440-640-eec-language-and-literacy-course/learning-module -1/module-11/consider%20the%20walls.pdf.

OECD (Organisation for Economic Co-operation and Development). (2002) *Understanding the Brain: Towards a New Learning Science*. Paris: OECD Publishing.

Van Puyvelde, M., Staring, L., Schaffers, J., Rivas-Smits, C., Groenendijk, L., Smeyers, L., Collette, L., Schoofs, A., Van den Bossche, N. and McGlone, F. (2021) Why do we hunger for touch? The impact of daily gentle touch stimulation on maternal-infant physiological and behavioral regulation and resilience. *Infant Mental Health Journal*, 42(6), pp. 823–883. Available at: https://doi.org/10.1016/j.cobeha .2022.101129.

Zhou, L. and Li, F. (2020) A review of the largest online teaching in China for elementary and middle school students during the COVID-19 pandemic. *Best Evidence in Chinese Education*, 5(1), pp. 549–567. Available at: https://files.eric.ed.gov/fulltext/EJ1288065 .pdf.

Zhuo, L., Wu, Q., Le, H., Li, H., Zheng, L., Ma, G. and Tao, H. (2021) COVID-19-related intolerance of uncertainty and mental health among back-to-school students in Wuhan: the moderation effect of social support. *International Journal of Environmental Research and Public Health*, 18(3), pp. 1–11. Available at: https://doi.org/10.3390/ijerph18030981.

From an early childhood point of view, behaviours are fascinating! Behaviours are often at the centre of many regular and ongoing, as well as interesting and varied (and sometimes heated) discussions. In this chapter, we will explore how we develop (or could develop) our knowledge and understanding regarding human (and therefore children's) behaviours. In addition, we will consider how this can (or should) support our growing knowledge of brain development and early childhood.

'Behaviours' actually means everything we do and say. Unfortunately, in many areas of the world, the word, and the meaning behind the word 'behaviours' has narrowed:

> I use the word behaviours purposefully. I hope you will notice it has the letter 's' on the end. Behaviour is often used as a plural, but that is not actually accurate. We tend to say 'children's behaviour' meaning all-encompassing, everything, rather than the more linguistically correct 'behaviours'. Additionally, the word 'behaviours' encompasses our words, actions, deeds, manner and conduct – in all its possible permutations. Yet, oddly, the word 'behaviour' (minus the 's') has come to have a definite and definitive, negative undertone. When we say, 'we want to talk about children's behaviour', we usually assume, usually correctly, that this is behaviour that is unacceptable or 'misaligned'. In other words, we use the word 'behaviour' as an all-encompassing term for any so-called 'negative' behaviour.
>
> (Garvey, 2018: 96)

DOI: 10.4324/9781003154846-3

Let's look at this in a little more detail:

REFLECTIVE PRACTICE

Exploring Behaviour(s)

Think about your experiences to this point:

What do you think is the general understanding of the word 'behaviour'?
Why do you think that is?
How have you heard or witnessed the word 'behaviour' used?
Have you heard the word 'behaviour' used negatively?
Have you heard the word 'behaviour' used positively?
Why do you think that is?
Do you think this needs further reflection for you and/or in your own team/workplace?
Where else could you look for information?
Who might be able to help?
How could adopting the use of the term 'behaviours' help?
For example: your thinking/practice, your team/colleagues/ parents, etc.?
Any other thoughts?

I suspect we can all share experiences where 'behaviour(s)' has been used in a way that makes us feel uncomfortable. Hopefully, your reflections should help you to consider if, and where, further thought is needed. If we go back to the previous quote, we can clearly see that behaviours are so much more than just negative. Perhaps it is time we started to embrace the wider perspectives of what it is to be human, and appreciate all of our interesting, intriguing, and sometimes curious behaviours.

Interestingly, science also feels that behaviours are fascinating too. So much so that there is a whole 'arm' of science specifically exploring behaviours. In this chapter we will explore how understanding some of the knowledge in this area can support us in early childhood. We will concentrate particularly on the areas of anthropology and psychology. These sit within the arm of science known as the behavioural sciences (sometimes called social sciences). I know it might sound a little odd, but come with me on this journey of discovery – who knows what we might find out, and how that might support us in our work with young children.

The Science of Behaviours

Researchers in these fields are particularly interested in the actions and deeds of what it means to be human – in other words, behaviours. Kappes (2016: 1, *emphasis in original*) asks people to discuss their thoughts on this wide and diverse area of science:

> *Matteo M Galizzi is an Assistant Professor of Behavioural Science at the Department of Social Policy ...*
>
> What is Behavioural Science ...? It is the cross-disciplinary, open-minded science of understanding how people behave. It cross-fertilises and brings closer together insights and methods from a variety of fields and disciplines, from experimental and behavioural economics to social and cognitive psychology, from judgement and decision-making to marketing and consumer behaviour, from health and biology to neuroscience, from philosophy to happiness and wellbeing research.

The article goes on to say:

> Tara Reich is an Assistant Professor of Management studying organizational behaviour
>
> Behavioural science is the systematic study of human behaviour. Behavioural scientists … use observation, interviews, surveys, and experiments to develop and test theories that explain when and why individuals behave as they do.

For me, this sits very well with our ever-growing understanding of early childhood – a fusion of knowledge, built on a historical foundation of observations, with a sprinkling of wisdom from a diverse range of other sectors. Maria Montessori recognised the value of this, well over one hundred years ago:

> It is my belief that the thing which we should cultivate … is more the *spirit* than the mechanical skill of the scientist … [it is not about] simply the acquiring of the technique of science … [from] anthropologists, … experimental psychologists, … [we should] *direct them* [educators] toward the field of experimental science, teaching them to manage the various instruments with a certain degree of skill … to awaken in the mind and heart of the educator an *interest in natural phenomena.*
>
> (Montessori, 1912: 10, *emphasis in original*)

In other words, Montessori wholeheartedly believed that the skills and tools that a range of scientists use would be extremely beneficial in developing knowledge and understanding around early childhood.

Early Childhood - Links to Behavioural Sciences?

Let's explore this in a little more detail and see where we could possibly make some links. Let's look at if (and how) this can perhaps support our early childhood knowledge, understanding and skills. One of the things I love about writing books is the way research carries me down new paths to explore – this is particularly true of the arm of the behavioural sciences known as anthropology. For me, anthropology, always initially makes me think of Dr Kathy Reich's books and the associated TV show *Bones*.

However, both the books and the TV show are based on Kathy's work as a *forensic* anthropologist. This work usually focusses on finding clues and evidence to support legal proceedings, usually by investigating human remains and crime scenes, for example. The anthropology Maria Montessori rated so highly, and perhaps we need to consider in more detail in our quest to understand early childhood, is actually much wider. As Ingold explains:

> could we not simply say that anthropology is the study of people? There is much to be said for this, but it does not help us to distinguish anthropology from all the other disciplines that claim to study people... history and psychology... biology and bio-medicine...
>
> What truly distinguishes anthropology, I believe, is that it is not a study *of*... but a study *with*.... [Anthropologists] learn to see things (or hear them, or touch them) in the ways ... teachers and companions do... anthropology, does more than furnish us with knowledge *about* the world... It rather educates our *perception* of the world, and opens our eyes and minds to other possibilities."
>
> (Ingold, 2008: 82, *emphasis in original*)

I particularly like this explanation as I think it aligns beautifully with a genuinely child-centred approach. Let's consider the Ingold (2008: 82) quote in a slightly different way; it could be almost a 'blueprint' for developing understanding in the field of early childhood.

REFLECTIVE PRACTICE

Anthropology – Learning *with* and *from* Children?

This is an adapted version of the Ingold (2008) quote, replacing the 'anthropology' angle with an 'early childhood' one:

> What truly distinguishes learning about early childhood, is that it is not a study *of*, but a study *with*.

We, as adults, learn to see things, or hear or touch them in the way the child does.

Working with and alongside young children, as we learn about early childhood, educates our perceptions of the early childhood world, and opens our eyes and minds to other possibilities.

(Adapted from Ingold, 2008: 82, *emphasis in original*)

In other words, learning *with* children, opens up the endless possibilities of learning *from* children:

Now consider the following questions:

Do you feel there is a difference between learning *about* working with children, and learning *from* working with children?

Why do you think that?

What do you think are some of the key differences?

What knowledge/skills/understanding (KSU), etc. do you feel you have developed learning *from* working with children?

How did the KSU develop, for example:

Can you think of incidents that supported your development as a practitioner?

A specific child/family/building/team, etc.?

How do you think learning *from* working with children expands your KSU of the early childhood world?

Why do you think that is?

Anything else?

I suspect that your reflections have some interesting points regarding the learning *from* and/or *with* children. In addition, I would suggest that there are some clear links between what anthropologists do, and what we as practitioners do in our work with children. This then implies that understanding a little about anthropology could indeed be helpful to those of us interested in understanding the early childhood world. Let's just start with a little look at some anthropological definitions. (Do not worry too much about the language, we are going to explore it a little more shortly.)

Further research uncovers that anthropology is often divided into subfields, usually four:

> Brinton, 1892, proposed ... four subdivisions of anthropology:
>
> (1) Somatology (physical and experimental anthropology)
> (2) Ethnology (historic and analytic anthropology)
> (3) Ethnography (geographic and descriptive anthropology)
> (4) Archaeology (prehistoric and reconstructive anthropology).
>
> (Hicks, 2013: 755)

> Anthropology is by nature an interdisciplinary field. Its subfields are intertwined with many other social and natural sciences. One reason that anthropology remains a broad, four-field discipline, rather than splitting up, is that all anthropologists recognize the importance of the following concepts: *culture*, *cultural relativism* [context], *diversity*, *change*, and *holism* [holistic approaches].
>
> (Welsch and Vivanco, 2018, online version, [no page],
> *emphasis in original*)

Over time, the sub-fields have developed and now usually cover four main categories – physical, linguistic, social/cultural and archaeology. Hopefully, what is clear is, that, just as the many areas of early childhood are inextricably interlinked, it can also be easily seen how the anthropological disciplines overlap and interact with each other. It is around this point that words start to look more familiar, and that perhaps the links with the study of early childhood become slightly clearer. Let's explore this in a little more detail:

REFLECTIVE PRACTICE

Early Childhood – Links to Anthropology

The four subfields of anthropology can be broadly understood as:

(1) Physical/Biological anthropology – environments, diseases, evolution and our links to other primates/apes, similarities and differences, behaviours, diet and nutrition, impact of stress, etc.
(2) Linguistic anthropology – language, communication (including the impact on our social interactions), etc.
(3) Social/Cultural anthropology – how we live and understand the world, interactions, characteristics, social lives, etc.
(4) Archaeology – past and historical human culture, etc.

Do not worry too much about the titles – concentrate more on the wider explanations.

Now let's turn our thinking to early childhood:

What springs to mind when you look at each of the subfields?
What links do you think of?
Where do you see links to understanding early childhood development?
Where do you see links to understanding behaviours?
Where do you see links to understanding brain development?
Any other thoughts/anything else?

Hopefully, you can see where this is going – and the reason for including anthropology in a book about young children, and in a chapter about behaviours. For me, the language and terms we have been discussing here take us right back to the main focus of this book – and back to neuroscience and early childhood. The subfields of physical, language, social and cultural anthropology show clear and direct correlations to our early childhood areas of development. It is also easy to see the links with our early childhood understanding of behaviours. Finally, the links to neuroscience and healthy brain development, discussed throughout this book, are also evident.

The 'anthropological' language of relationships, environments, and interactions, stress, diet, diseases, language and communication, characteristics, understanding of the world, diversity, links to culture, past experiences and holistic approaches are terms wholly familiar in the early childhood world. Can we then take this further, and put anthropological methods and understanding into child-centred approaches?

Child-Centred Anthropology

One of the key ways to collect anthropological research about a particular group is a research method known as ethnography (mentioned in the earlier Hicks, 2013, quote). The word 'ethnography' comes from Greek words meaning 'people' and 'I write'. In other words – 'I write about people.' This is known as 'qualitative' research:

> [Qualitative research is] research using methods such as participant observation or case studies which result in a narrative, descriptive account of a setting or practice.
>
> (Parkinson and Drislane, 2011 [no page])

In other words, qualitative, ethnographical research is using observations and case studies, for example, which give a description, or tell a story/stories which help to gain knowledge and understanding. This is beginning to all sound very familiar to our early childhood world. Allen (2017) offers a helpful explanation:

> Ethnography is both a process (e.g., one does ethnography) and a product (e.g., one writes an ethnography).

In doing ethnography, an ethnographer actively participates in the group in order to gain an insider's perspective of the group and to have experiences similar to the group members.

In writing ethnography, an ethnographer creates an account of the group based on this participation, interviews with group members, and an analysis of group documents and artifacts.

(Allen, 2017, online version [no page])

Again, this fits with our understanding and practice in early childhood. For example,

Observations and learning journeys could be classed as types of ethnography.

Practitioners writing observations, developing learning journeys/children's stories, using current documentation to support learning, and generally being involved in the group, could be classed as ethnographers.

Documentation – policies, procedures, legal, good practice guidance, etc.

As well as historical, recent, and ongoing research, articles, books, etc. (whether by us as individuals, collectively as a group/sector – or by academics and scholars who have studied the early childhood field).

The resources we provide could be classed as 'artifacts' of today's childhood. (Particularly as some of these are timeless and much-loved over many generations, or may appear suddenly, or change and/or develop over time, for example.)

In other words, ethnography is (or perhaps *should* be) a key part of what we believe to be valuable, crucial, and effective early childhood practice. For example:

We promote the importance of being actively engaged with children.
We talk with, and to, children to better understand their thoughts, feelings, ideas, and so on.
We have specific documentation.
Resources offer insights into the world of children.

Therefore, an early childhood ethnography could be explained as how we use our observations, discussions, documentation, planning, activities, and resources, etc. And – how, together, all of these things develop our overarching knowledge and understanding, and create a narrative, or story, of the experiences and lives of the children. It therefore should be no real surprise to discover that there is a wealth of anthropological and ethnographical research directly relating to children and childhood.

Levine (2007: 247) suggests that ethnography is a vital tool in the context of a constantly shifting field such as childhood:

> An ethnographic study of childhood … is a descriptive account, based on … observations and interviews, of the lives, activities, and experiences of children in a particular place and time, and of the contexts – social, cultural, institutional, economic – that make sense of their behavior there and then.

He concludes that:

> The ethnography of childhood, then, is based on the premise … that the conditions and shape of childhood tend to vary … from one population to another, are sensitive to population-specific contexts, and [need] … detailed knowledge of the socially and culturally organized contexts that give them meaning.

To put it another way, Levine (2007) is asking us to consider that children's behaviours (in the widest sense of the word) are influenced by everything that is happening around them – at that moment in time. Which of course, absolutely ties in with our early childhood approach to child-led, child-centred practice.

In other words:

We use our observations and knowledge of the children in the here and now.
This then adds to previous knowledge and understanding:
Either our own knowledge and understanding of working with children.
Or the things we have read, researched, or studied, for example.
And so, over time, we build a narrative (story) unique to the children in the here and now.

Which, in turn, influences future generations – as our collective knowledge and understanding builds and develops. Therefore our pedagogy, practice and skills build on what has gone before, *and* what is happening now, and so develop continuously. If we think back to earlier discussions in this chapter, Maria Montessori's work is based on her observations of children at that time. Our understanding has grown and developed and builds on that work. We might not consider ourselves great researchers (or ethnographers) like Montessori, but our observations build on, and add to that continuously growing knowledge, and we should celebrate that contribution to research – no matter how small.

Levine (2007) also asks us to be mindful to the context (or environments) that children find themselves in – the social, cultural, institutional, and economic environments that have an influence on, and impact on, children, as they grow up. Again, this makes sense to our early childhood understanding. In addition, this links very closely with Bronfenbrenner's 'Ecological Model' (1977, 1979, 1992) which we will explore in more depth in a later chapter.

Let's just consider two ways this could support the ongoing and continuous development and reflections of our collective understanding. We could use Levine's definitions, or we could use the language of Personal, Social and Emotional Development (PSED).

The *SEAD (Social and Emotional Aspects of Development) Guidance for Practitioners* document (2008: 5) offers a useful explanation and overview:

Personal, Social and Emotional Development (PSED) are three building blocks of future success in life. They are closely linked to each other and often bracketed together as one area of learning and development.

Personal development (Being me) – how we come to understand who we are and what we can do, how we look after ourselves.
Social development (Being social) – how we come to understand ourselves in relation to others, how we make friends, understand the rules of society and behave towards others.
Emotional development (Having feelings) – how we come to understand our own and others' feelings and develop our ability to 'stand in someone else's shoes' and see things from their point of view, referred to as empathy.

We explored environments in the previous chapter. However, let's consider this in relation to contexts – why are environments and contexts important in our quest for better understanding and knowledge, and how does (or could) this influence our practice and pedagogy?

REFLECTIVE PRACTICE

Childhood Contexts/Environments

Consider the grid(s) – how have contexts/environments changed, or how might they change, for a specific population of children? These are just three timeframes as examples – the 1800s, 1930s–1950s and now.

Think about what you would expect children to experience (or not) in the different contexts and timeframes.

For example – how might the 'social' context be different in the 1800s compared to now, or the 'institutional' context differ from the 1800s to the 1930s–1950s, for example.

In any generation, there will of course be some children with vastly different experiences to others – this is about knowledge of the 'general' population. What do you *think* it would be/is like for *most* children? Likewise, if you're not sure what to put, do not worry about filling every box, this is just a general overview for reflection purposes.

You could choose to do either Grid 1 (using Levine's environments) or Grid 2 (using early childhood PSED environments), or you could do both, and reflect on the similarities or differences in the grids.

Childhood Contexts			
Grid 1	A child growing up in the 1800s	A child growing up in the 1930s–1950s	A child growing up now
Social: Friendships, Relationships, Community, for example.			

Cultural: *Equality, Diversity, Movement of people, for example.*			
Institutional: *Education, Health, Social Care, for example.*			
Economic: *Home, Food, Shelter, Society, Poverty, Wealth, for example.*			
Grid 2	*A child growing up in the 1800s*	*A child growing up in the 1930s–1950s*	*A child growing up now*
Personal Development: *Being me*			

Social Development: *Being social*			
Emotional Development: *Having feelings*			

It should be fairly easy to see why we need to consider (and understand) the importance of the contexts and environments that children find themselves in. Furthermore, it should be clear how these impact on childhood and have a direct influence on children's behaviours – and indeed brain development. For example, a child growing up in the 1800s could be in employment (in the mines, or sweeping chimneys, for example). In addition, children in the 1800s might not have access to appropriate health, social care, and education services. It then becomes easy to see how these environments and contexts are going to impact on behaviours (and, of course, healthy brain development).

Of course, there are other environments and contexts we could add too. How does childhood differ if you grow up in a different part of the country or world? We could compare rural (countryside), coastal (seaside), and urban (towns/cities), for example. We could consider the hot countries and the cold countries, or the richer nations and the poorer nations – the contexts and environments are endless. However, they all have one thing in common – they will all influence the lives of the children who live there, and as adults, it is our duty to take notice.

Listening to Children

In terms of understanding brain development, if we truly want to understand childhood, and truly make a difference to children's lives, then we need to listen to what children are telling us. Whilst we cannot see inside children's heads, we can see brain developments happening in real-time. The often-quoted Mehrabian (1981) tells us that communication is 7 per cent the words we use, 38 per cent tone of voice and 55 per cent non-verbal. This aligns well with our knowledge in early childhood, and again shows us the importance of observations.

Children are very good at communicating with us and showing us exactly what their brains are doing. Almost like a mirror to the outside world, their inner thoughts, feelings, and opinions are reflected in their behaviours (in the widest sense of the word). If we consider babies, or children with English as an additional language, or children who are non-verbal, they often use very little language to show us what they are thinking and feeling. Likewise, all children communicate with us in a range of different ways. This is clear to anyone who has joined in a splashing-in-puddles game with a four-year-old, or tried to put an unhappy toddler into a pushchair, or change the nappy of a baby desperate to continue crawling.

The key here is, how do we firstly ensure we are 'listening' to what children are telling us, and secondly, show we are acting on what we are being told? Our observations, the way we engage with children, and build knowledge of them as individuals, are all ways in which we show children we are truly listening. In addition, by listening in a range of ways, we can begin to interpret the array of behaviours we see. Furthermore, we can begin to understand how the contexts and environments are influencing the child/ren. Dickins and Williams (2017: 3) explain that listening is:

An active process of receiving (hearing and observing), interpreting and responding to communication – it includes all the senses and emotions and is not limited to the spoken word.

They go on to say:

An ongoing part of tuning in to all young children as individuals in their every-day lives. Understanding listening in this way is key to providing an environment in which all young children, including babies, feel confident, safe and power-ful, ensuring they have the time and space to express themselves in whatever form suits them.

Montgomery (2009: 6) reminds us that we need to ensure that we actively involve children and listen to, and value, their feelings, thoughts, prefer-ences, and opinions:

> This analytical approach to children's lives might best be described as 'child-centred' or 'child-focused' anthropology and it demands the use of children as primary informants and focuses on children's voices and children's agency [being able to make choices and decisions].

In other words, if we want to know and understand about early childhood, then children are best placed to show us what that looks like. That childhood should be viewed from the child's perspective, is of course, very recognis-able. The beliefs that children should be the main narrators of their own childhood, have a voice and be able to make choices and decisions, are again familiar, and central to early childhood practice.

Whilst child-centred anthropology and ethnography might be new areas for consideration, they also feel comfortable and familiar to our early childhood world. The theory, practices and even language align well with our much-loved, research-informed, evidence-based, sector-wide view of early childhood. By taking on board some of the wider principles, such as the importance of context and place and time (the here and now), as well as familiar concepts such as children's voices, we can begin to understand what it feels like for children now.

What then strikes me is that it becomes clear that there are some strong links here to the UN Convention on the Rights of the Child (UNCRC, 1989). Woven into child-centred anthropology, ethnography and, of course, our early childhood practices, is the language of rights: the right to be listened to and heard, the right to express views, thoughts and opinions and be taken seriously, the right to play, the rights of friendship, culture, and access to information, for example.

In addition, the far-reaching rights around disability and inclusion, edu-cation, health and wellbeing, safety and protection from abuse, poverty, violence, war, etc., are an integral part of our society, as well as a crucial part of the laws, regulations and documentation that underpins our work across the sector.

It can be helpful to remember:

UNCRC applies to all children (Article 1), and that all adults must uphold the rights.

There are 4 Core Principles – they apply across all the other rights:

Non-discrimination

Best interests of the child

Life, survival, and development

Respect for the views of the child

In addition, there are three overarching main themes, often referred to as the 3 Ps

Participation – Provision – Protection

In other words, in everything we do and provide we must ensure children are protected, supported to develop, and reach their potential. Furthermore, the UNCRC (1989) expects us to understand, advocate, and respect difference and diversity, inclusion, involvement, the child's views, and opinions, etc. And to do that, we need to listen to children. We do this by understanding, respecting, and acting on whatever it is they are trying to tell us, through whichever means of communication (including behaviours) the child/ren use. Let's consider this in a little more detail and look at how this might support early childhood practice.

REFLECTIVE PRACTICE

UNCRC (1989) – Listening to Children (Part 1)

Consider the day-to-day experiences we have with children. For example:

How do children tell us, or show us, their thoughts, feelings, opinions, etc.?

What might you expect to see or hear?

How do we know when children are worried, scared, or concerned?

How do we know when children are excited, happy, or interested?

UNCRC (1989) – Listening to Children (Part 2)

Now consider, how do we show children we are listening to their uniqueness, their thoughts, feeling and opinions, etc.?
You might want to consider:

The environments (physical and emotional).
The documentation – legal, policies, procedures, etc.
Practice and pedagogy – the relationships and teaching, how we support children to grow, develop and flourish.

For example, you could consider:

How do we support babies, non-verbal children, or children who speak other languages?
How do we support children with disabilities, or additional needs?
How do we support children from a range of families, such as refugee/asylum- seeker, adoptive, same-sex or traveller families, for example?
How do we support the different age ranges – such as toddlers, or four-year-olds, for example?

In other words – how do we embed the UNCRC (1989) into daily practice?

	Participation	Provision	Protection
Non-discrimination (Equality, inclusion, diversity, etc.)			

Best interests of the child (Making decisions, etc.)			
Life, survival and development (Be protected, achieve potential, etc.)			
Respect for the views of the child (Thoughts, feelings and opinions, etc.)			

I suspect it is very clear how the UNCRC has a central role in developing and informing our practices across the early childhood sector. So, to summarise this section – anthropology, child-centred anthropology, and ethnography, all use language we are familiar with. There are structures from other disciplines that feel recognisable and could so easily be used in our world. That behaviours are more than just negative and are influenced by a whole host of things, including environments and contexts, is clear. Finally, children have rights, which underpin laws and legislation – but equally places a duty on adults to respect, involve, and listen to children.

My question then would be – do we use this knowledge and understanding effectively when we are considering the influences on children's learning, development, and growing brain?

For example (in no particular order):

Do we consider if the policies and procedures we develop are truly child-centred?
Do we take on board the importance of the environments and social, cultural, institutional, economic, and political contexts?
Do we consider the language we use?
Do we learn *with* and *from* children?
Do we consider our knowledge of brain development and neuroscience?
Could using terms such as 'behavioural sciences', 'anthropology', and 'ethnography' more widely, influence and support the sector? Would this offer improved recognition, support and value for the work we do?

And, for all of these questions – if not, why not?
This of course relies on us being able to communicate our ideas, thoughts, and feelings, whatever our age, and that leads us rather nicely into psychology.

Psychology

Psychology is of course one of the arms of the behavioural sciences that has clear links to behaviours. The British Psychological Society (BPS) offers:

> Psychology is the scientific study of the mind and how it dictates and influences our behaviour, from communication and memory to thought and emotion. …
> the study of human behaviour – and the thoughts, feelings, and motivations behind it – through observation, measurement, and testing.
> (British Psychological Society, 2022, *emphasis in original*)

While initially we might think of the unhelpful and stereotypical image of lying on a couch with a Sigmund Freud–type conversation going on, the BPS quote offers some very familiar language:

> Behaviour, communication, memory, emotion, thoughts, feelings, motivations.

And immediately the links between psychology and early childhood are clear. In addition, psychology, like anthropology, has several 'branches' covering specific areas. These include cognitive psychology, developmental psychology, and social psychology, for example, and again, this language feels very familiar to our early childhood world.

There are also other branches that may offer some useful information in terms of our early childhood understanding. Educational psychology is perhaps already familiar and is often used to support children and families experiencing difficulties. In addition, health psychology (sometimes called behavioural medicine), looks at how socioeconomics, backgrounds and behaviours influence the health of humans (including children). Personally, I find this one interesting as it covers areas such as family life, poverty, inequality and discrimination, abuse, and the impact of stress, for example. This then links to our discussions elsewhere in this book and the impacts of toxic stress, especially when there are no adults present to buffer the impacts – which of course then links to our behaviours:

> No behavior sits in a vacuum, and one behavior can greatly affect what happens next.
>
> (Dolan and Galizzi, 2015: 1)

Overall, psychology is about the mind, and how we process information. Of course, the information we receive comes from a variety of sources, and can be useful, helpful, and relevant, or not, as the case may be. This is about what influences how we think, our emotions and feelings, and of course how all of this interlinks and influences our communication, memories, behaviours and so on.

REFLECTIVE PRACTICE

Links to Psychology (Part 1)

Think about a time when you have had a difficult situation (it doesn't have to be a big, scary stressful situation, unless of course you want it to be – just something that was more stressful than normal).

Now consider how this situation influenced your:
Behaviour
Communication
Emotions/feelings
Thoughts
Motivation
Memory
Anything else you want to add?

Your reflections should clearly show how psychology helps us to understand human behaviours, and should show how our processing of information influences a whole host of other areas. Then, thinking back to the earlier Reflective Practice exercise 'Stress, Stressors and Support' –

What did the people around you do to help?

This, of course, is where the 'buffers' come in – a word, a touch, an expression, an offer of help and so on – sometimes so small they are hardly noticeable. However, these gestures are vital in that they help us to regulate our feelings, thoughts, and behaviours. I am sure you can guess what question comes next?

If this is how we feel as grownups, then how do children feel?

Hmmm… there are many angles we could explore further here, but as we are specifically looking at psychology and behaviours, perhaps an interesting area to explore might be transitional objects – objects that can be used as buffers – and the important role they play regulating feelings. In other words, I wonder how often we stop to consider the importance, relevance, and signifi-cance of the transitional object – the well-worn, much-loved, much-travelled, teddy, a favourite toy, or quite literally the 'blankie' (or the so-called security blanket). I am sure you have all seen the panicked, desperate messages and photos on social media when a deeply treasured teddy, worn and tatty with years of love, is suddenly missing. Thankfully, social media comes into its own and responds swiftly. Often teddy and owner are quickly reunited, the story faithfully followed by kind humans desperately trying to help. I wonder how important this actually is. Let's explore this a little:

REFLECTIVE PRACTICE

Links to Psychology (Part 2)

Linking back to the previous reflective exercise – Links to Psychology (Part 1) – imagine you are dealing with the difficult situation, someone steps forward and tells you that before you can continue, you must leave your handbag/watch/scarf/phone/wallet/jewellery on a shelf or in a cupboard.

How do you think this would influence your:
Behaviour?
Communication?
Emotions/feelings?
Thoughts?
Motivation?
Memory?
Anything else you want to add?

Hmm, yes, I know, you are already there.... I am sure you can guess what question comes next:

If this is how we feel as grownups, then how do children feel?

If we go back to the lost teddy or blankie for a moment. I wonder how many of those kind humans on social media stop to think of the gravity of the situation from a small child's point of view. Do they wonder as to the very real significance of the object – and why that is? Do they consider the neuroscience behind the transitional object? How the touch, smell, sound, sight or even taste of something makes us feel safe – or indeed not, as the case may be? How certain things help to quell the cortisol when we feel anxious? In other words, how teddies (Zeedyk, 2013) and other important objects help with self-regulation:

> We wouldn't remove a wheelchair from a student, yet we often deny young people their own coping mechanisms through unintended consequences of wider systems and policies.
>
> (Morewood, 15 March 2019, para 11)

And I wonder if anyone considers how we all use articles to help us feel safe. Does that include adults, I hear you ask – well, lucky socks or scarf, anyone? Perhaps a favourite outfit that makes us feel invincible, or a watch or piece of jewellery to stay connected to a loved one. That faded cushion that still sits on the sofa, or the ancient bag that comes on every holiday. As adults, these objects might be used as a lucky charm, mascot, or talisman, but it stems from reminders of times when we felt safe – or reminders of loved ones who helped us to feel safe. In addition, there have also been several studies considering the role of the smart phone as the modern-day transitional object (Konok, 2017; Shay, 2020). Kelly Roberts, EYFS Lead at East Hunsbury Primary School, offers the following reflection on the importance of transitional objects.

For the Little People, It's the Little Things

As a teacher and a student of psychology, transitional periods have always been of interest. How can we help the children and parents to feel happier and more at ease during these times?

Early in my career I was lucky enough to be a part of a European project focusing on the importance of building emotional literacy in children, working alongside educators and psychologists from Spain, Romania, Croatia and Italy. It was truly a wonderful project and taught me many things. One of my key takeaways was the importance of gifts within these cultures. Not the huge, expensive, technical items that make up many of our own children's Christmas lists but small, often handmade, thoughtful talismans. Something small that can be held in a small hand and squeezed tight, something to say, "I see you; I care."

Ready Confetti

During one of our transition events, visiting nursery children are given a small packet of "Ready Confetti", it has a short verse on the front,

Sprinkle this confetti under your pillow the night before school.
It will help you to have sweet dreams and be ready for a day of fun!

It shows the children that we recognise potential anxieties and look forward to having a lovely day with them.

Paired Hearts

Inspired by those in hospitals during the pandemic, I crocheted 120 paired hearts for our new starters, one for them to hold and one for their parent. I explained to the children that when they were missing their parents, they could squeeze it and they would feel the cuddle. They absolutely loved them, and they were used frequently in the first half term. In fact, many still adorn their book bags as I sit writing this on my last day of term.

Worry Worms

For the transition from reception to year 1, I also create "Worry Worms" for the children alongside another short poem,

Moving to year 1 is exciting not scary,
It's perfectly normal to feel a bit wary...
I am your little worry worm, keep me close, keep me near,
When a worry pops into your head whisper in my ear,
I will take away your worry, so you have nothing to fear.

To see two of my former pupils with them in their hands two years later says it all really.

These are my reflections on some such objects that I have used to support transitions. Many of these ideas are inspired by wonderful people from across the internet but this is how they have worked for me and my lovely children. Show them you care, don't spend a fortune, and get crafty if you can. Little things matter to little people!

[If you would like to find out more and see photos of some of the things discussed, you can connect with Kelly on Twitter @ KellyJRoberts88]

Whatever the object, it connects with our senses, sends messages throughout the body and brain, and tells our parasympathetic nervous system (see Chapter 1 for more) that everything is right with the world. After all, we wouldn't be snuggling up with an old cushion or smiling at photos on our phones if we were being chased by a lion. Whatever our preference, I suspect we all have transitional objects that support us in dealing with situations that make us worried or anxious and assist with self-regulation (and we will come back to regulation in Chapter 6).

Hopefully, this chapter has helped us to explore some of the wider scientific areas that have influenced our understanding of early childhood, and the associated influences on brain development. I wholeheartedly believe we should acknowledge and embrace this wider multi-disciplinary research. I strongly believe that it can provide a wealth of knowledge, understanding and support to the early childhood sector. In addition, it might be worth considering how these other fields are perceived, and how it sometimes feels the early childhood world is perceived: I wonder if there is any learning to be had from that too.

Unfortunately, there is not room to investigate all the research here. As always, do explore the bibliography as a starting point for more on psychology, ethnography, anthropology, and the anthropology of childhood – you never know what you might find. Or, as Bock, Gaskins and Lancy (2008: 5) explain:

> disciplinary boundaries provide comfort zones for the members of each discipline. We can easily remain within those boundaries and focus on the relevant body of literature. Yet ... the benefits of exploring the literature of other subfields and integrating data and theoretical perspectives will bring benefits [and] foster exchange and interaction.

Chapter Reflection

Thinking back over this chapter, consider the various elements (sections, quotes, reflective exercises, terminology, etc.). Are there any elements that:

Were particularly useful?
Need re-reading, or more thought or reflection?
You want to look up and/or explore further?

Any other thoughts or reflections?

Bibliography

The following are books, articles, web pages, organisations, documents, etc. that I have found useful (online versions, all accessed 20 July 2022). Some are directly referenced in this chapter – some are included as valuable sources of background reading that might be helpful. See also web resources at the end of Chapter 1.

Allen, M. (2017) *The Sage Encyclopedia of Communication Research Methods* (Vols. 1–4). Thousand Oaks, CA: SAGE Publications, Inc. Available at: https://methods.sagepub.com/reference/the-sage-encyclopedia-of-communication-research-methods/i4910.xml.

American Anthropological Association (2022) Available at: https://www.americananthro.org/AdvanceYourCareer/Content.aspx?ItemNumber=2150.

Bock, J., Gaskins, S. and Lancy, D. F. (2008) A four-field anthropology of childhood. *Anthropology News*, 49(4), pp. 4–5.

Brinton. D. G. (1892) Proposed classification and international nomenclature for the anthropological sciences. In: E. W. Putnam, ed. *Proceedings of the American Association for the Advancement of Science for the 41st Meeting, held at Rochester, NY.* Salem, MA: Salem Press, pp. 257–258. Available at: http://www.jstor.org/stable/658363.

British Psychological Society (2022) Available at: http://www.0711zp.com/bps/public/what-is-psychology/.

Bronfenbrenner, U. (1977) Toward an experimental ecology of human development. *American Psychologist*, 32, pp. 513–531. Available at: https://psycnet.apa.org/doi/10.1037/0003-066X.32.7.513.

Bronfenbrenner, U. (1979) *The Ecology of Human Development.* Cambridge, MA: Harvard University Press.

Bronfenbrenner, U. (1992) *Ecological Systems Theory.* London: Jessica Kingsley Publishers.

Convention on the Rights of the Child (1989) Treaty no. 27531. *United Nations Treaty Series*, 1577, pp. 3–178. Available at: https://www.ohchr.org/en/instruments-mechanisms/instruments/convention-rights-child.

Department for Children, Schools, and Families (DCSF) (2008) *SEAD (Social and Emotional Aspects of Development): Guidance for Practitioners Working in the Foundation Stage.* Nottingham: DCSF Publications. Available at: https://www.foundationyears.org.uk/wp-content/uploads/2011/10/SEAD_Guidance_For_Practioners.pdf.

Dolan, P. and Galizzi, M. M. (2015) Like ripples on a pond: behavioral spillovers and their implications for research and policy. *Journal of Economic Psychology*, 47, pp. 1–16. Available at: https://doi.org/10.1016/j.joep.2014.12.003.

Dickins, M. and Williams, L. (2017) *Listening as a Way of Life: Listening to Young Disabled Children*. London: National Children's Bureau.

Garvey, D. (2018) *Nurturing Personal, Social and Emotional Development in Early Childhood: A Practical Guide to Understanding Brain Development and Young Children's Behaviour*. London: Jessica Kingsley Publishers.

Hicks, D. (2013) Four-field anthropology: charter myths and time warps from St. Louis to Oxford. *Current Anthropology*, 54(6), pp. 753–763. Available at: https://www.journals.uchicago.edu/doi/full/10.1086/673385.

Ingold, T. (2008) Anthropology is not ethnography. *Proceedings of the British Academy*, 154(11), pp. 69–92.

Kappes, H. (2016) *What is Behavioural Science at the LSE?* London: London School of Economics. Available at: https://blogs.lse.ac.uk/behaviouralscience/2016/05/24/what-is-behavioural-science-at-the-lse/.

Kehoe, A. B. (2013) *Humans: An Introduction to Four-Field Anthropology*. Abingdon: Routledge.

Konok, V., Pogány, Á. and Miklósi, Á. (2017) Mobile attachment: separation from the mobile phone induces physiological and behavioural stress and attentional bias to separation-related stimuli. *Computers in Human Behavior*, 71, pp. 228–239. Available at: https://doi.org/10.1016/j.chb.2017.02.002.

Lancy, D. F. (2014) *The Anthropology of Childhood: Cherubs, Chattel, Changelings*. Cambridge: Cambridge University Press.

Levine, R. A. (2007) Ethnographic studies of childhood: a historical overview. *American Anthropologist*, 109(2), pp. 247–260. Available at: https://www.jstor.org/stable/4496639.

Mehrabian, A. (1981) *Silent Messages: Implicit Communication of Emotions and Attitudes*. Belmont: Wadsworth.

Montessori, M. (1912) *The Montessori Method: Scientific Pedagogy as Applied to Child Education in 'The Children's Houses' with Additions and Revisions by the Author* (A. E. George, Trans.). Cambridge, MA: Robert Bentley.

Montgomery, H. (2009) *An Introduction to Childhood: Anthropological Perspectives on Children's Lives.* Chichester: Wiley-Blackwell.

Morewood, G. (2019) Why understanding our own stress matters. *Optimus Education.* [blog] 15 March. Available at: https://blog.optimus-education.com/why-understanding-our-own-stress-matters.

Parkinson, G. and Drislane, R. (2011) *Qualitative research.* In *Online Dictionary of the Social Sciences.* Available at: https://bitbucket.icaap.org/dict.pl?term=qualitative%20research.

Shay, J. M. (2020) *Attachment Theory and Smartphone Use: Are Smartphones Transitional Objects?* (Doctoral dissertation, University of Georgia). Available at: https://esploro.libs.uga.edu/esploro/outputs/doctoral/attachment-theory-and-smartphone-use-are-smartphones-transitional-objects/9949365541702959.

Welsch, R. L. and Vivanco, L. A. (2018) *Asking Questions about Cultural Anthropology: A Concise Introduction.* 2nd edn. New York: Oxford University Press Inc.

Zeedyk, S. (2013) *Sabre Tooth Tigers and Teddy Bears: The Connected Baby Guide to Understanding Attachment.* Dundee: Suzanne Zeedyk Ltd.

I am sure no one interested in how small children develop and flourish would argue with the title of this chapter – Play Matters! Of course it does, I hear you shout enthusiastically… Play Matters! It is a simple statement that any champion of early childhood would agree with emphatically. Without question, a chapter on play definitely needs including in this book. However, as well as a book about early childhood, this is a book about neuroscience and the science behind brain development. Can the two *really* go together? Can science *really* help us to understand *why* play matters? Are there areas other than early childhood where we can look for evidence? Maybe the title of this chapter should be – Does play matter, and if so, why? (OK, maybe not so catchy.)

What Is Play?

We will shortly explore some key play theorists' definitions, but before that, it might be helpful to consider what play means to us.

REFLECTIVE PRACTICE

Play is….

Consider the title of this exercise, and finish the sentence:

    Play is……………………………………………………………………

DOI: 10.4324/9781003154846-4

In other words – what does play mean to *you*? What is *your* definition of play?

When you have jotted down a few thoughts, consider the following questions:

What key words are included in your definition?
What do you think influences your definition?
Childhood – home/school, etc.?
How does this influence your definition?
Why do you think that is?
Family, cultural background and community, etc.?
How does this influence your definition?
Why do you think that is?
Career – training, research, experience and so on?
How does this influence your definition?
Why do you think that is?
Anything else?

As part of the research for this book, I asked children I know, and I also asked this question of friends and colleagues (in person and on Twitter). I asked people to ask children in their work or personal lives to share their views on play, or to finish the sentence, 'What is play.....?'
Play is.....

Play is messy (Aged 2)
Playing is super fun, I like playing in the rain (Aged 3)
I just love to play; I love to play with my toys and play outside (Aged 5)
Play is time with my friends (Aged 8)

There were so many comments that took my breath away. The answers were interesting, insightful, and full of childhood understanding. Supported by a highly sensitive and tuned-in adult, this message comes from a 3-year-old, and is one we could all do with remembering:

Relaxing in the hammock with a little girl during today's session, she asked me to
"Come and play with me"
[I replied] "But I don't know how to play, what should I do?"

She gave me a daisy,
"Just hold this, go for a walk, and take it on an adventure"....
(Tweet from Lea Archer: AKA Free-Range Forest @LeaLeaLemon)

The History of Play

Now we have a personal definition of play, and some thoughts on how children see play, let's consider some of the more famous (and maybe not so famous) quotes from some prominent play and child development theorists. Well over 100 years ago, German educator, and the founder of kindergarten (the garden of children), Friedrich Froebel truly understood the power of play.

Play is the purest, most spiritual activity ... typical of human life
It gives ... joy, freedom, contentment, inner and outer rest, peace with the world. It holds the sources of all that is good with the world.
(Froebel, 1887: 55)

On the Shoulders of Giants

The very language we use in early childhood is rooted in history. The term pedagogy, for example, comes from the Ancient Greek words for children (paides), play (paidia), and education (paideia):

> The central aim of pedagogy (paidagogia) is to encourage learning as a form of play (paidia).
>
> (Krentz, 1998: 205)

Whilst the word 'pedagogy' is not always used collectively (or indeed comfortably) across the early childhood sector, the idea of the importance of early childhood, and learning and development through play, is certainly wholly embraced.

I often say that in the early childhood profession, we stand on the shoulders of giants. We have over 2000 years of history to call on, and that gives us what Nutbrown and Clough (2014: 3) call "a 'rootedness' to our work".

Year	Quote	Reference
35–97 (AD)	The time gained in childhood is clear profit to the period of youth. Let us not therefore waste the earliest years.	Quintilian (translation by Butler, 1963: 29)
1762	Let him be taken every day, far out into the fields. There, let him run about, play, fall down a hundred times a day; the oftener the better, as he will soon learn to get up again by himself.	Worthington, 1889: 41 (quoting Jean-Jacques Rousseau)
1842	Where are these rational practices to be taught and acquired? Not within the four walls of a bare building, in which formality predominates .... But in the nursery, play-ground, fields, gardens, workshops ... museums and class-rooms. ...The facts collected from all these sources will be concentrated, explained, discussed, made obvious to all, and shown in their direct application to practice in all the business of life.	Owen, 1842: 97
1887	Play is the highest form of child development. Play at this time [early childhood] is not trivial, it is highly serious and of deep significance.	Froebel, 1887: 54 Froebel, 1887: 55

1933	Let us turn now to the role of play and its influence on a child's development. I think it is enormous. In play a child is always above his average age, above his daily behavior; in play it is as though he were a head taller than himself. As in the focus of a magnifying glass, play contains all developmental tendencies in a condensed form; in play it is as though the child were trying to jump above the level of his normal behavior.	Vygotsky, 1933: 875 Vygotsky, 1933: 890
1937	If we were asked to mention one supreme psychological need of the young child, the answer would have to be "play" – the opportunity for free play in all its various forms. Play is the child's means of living and of understanding life.	Issacs, 1948: 149
1949	He becomes a man by means of his hands, by means of his experience, first through play, then through work.	Montessori, 1949: 37
1955	First and foremost, then, all play is a voluntary activity. Play to order is no longer play.	Huizinga, 1955: 1094

Over 2000 years ago, Plato (429–347 B.C.E.), and his student Aristotle (384–322 B.C.E.), considered play an important part of early childhood learning and development. As we travel through history, Jean-Jacques Rousseau (1712–1778) and Johann Pestalozzi (1746–1827) were amongst the first to speak out on the belief we should listen to children and be guided by their curiosity and interests.

Margaret McMillan (1860–1931) worked with her sister Rachel to develop outdoor nursery provision and the first teacher training college. McMillan talked of the need to look holistically at our work with children, and understood the importance of taking the home environment into account. John Dewey (1859–1952) would also add further to what we now call a child-led approach.

Russian psychologist Lev Vygotsky (1896–1934) was very clear on his beliefs around the importance of play. Equally, Dr Maria Montessori is also highly regarded for her belief in learning through play and experience. In the quote in the grid, Montessori uses the term 'man' to mean the species, or human. This quote is often shortened to the slightly easier to remember, "play is the work of the child". Susan Sutherland-Isaacs (1885–1948) believed in the importance of early education, and that any setting where young children are, should be developed on love, kindness, and relationships. Whilst Paolo Freire (1921–1997) talked of the importance of conversations, community, and the significance of real experiences.

It is easy to see how our play-based approach to early childhood has developed. As we move through history, other voices join the call for recognition of the importance of early childhood. Names such as Athey, Bandura, Bronfenbrenner, Bruner, Donaldson, Erikson, Freud, Goldschmied, Katz, Laevers, Malaguzzi, Maslow, Parten, Piaget, and Steiner are just some you may recognise. (A quick internet search will bring up plenty of places to explore these and many more.) These, and other giants of the early childhood world, added their thoughts to the ever-growing knowledge and understanding of play and child development.

And it wasn't just education and early childhood theorists. As Britain developed during the Industrial Revolution of the 1800s, philanthropists such as Robert Owen, George and Richard Cadbury, and Titus Salt understood the importance of learning by experience and learning by doing. Outdoor play and experiential learning featured heavily in the support and opportunities that were provided for the younger children of the families who worked in the factories and mills.

The history of play and early education during the Industrial Revolution in Britain is liberally sprinkled with various philanthropic and charitable endeavours by the educated, privileged and/or wealthy business men and women of the time. The research is plentiful. We learn of efforts to abolish child labour, improve health, and well-intentioned programmes to support education within the U.K. It is clear that the philanthropists of the time had a social and moral conscience in relation to their local communities. The disturbing history of how some of those developments came about is only now starting to be considered. We cannot talk of modern Britain, and the history of how early education was developed (and therefore financed), without acknowledging our appalling treatment of other nations.

As international travel became easier and global markets opened up, this funded the Industrial Revolution. Access to land in other countries brought access to crops. The raw materials of sugar, tea, coffee, cocoa, and cotton, for example, could be manufactured, monetised, and scaled up for huge profits, at devastating human cost overseas.

The great bulk of that essential raw material came from the Mississippi Valley and the "white gold" [cotton] of the Deep South was harvested by the black hands of enslaved Africans. In the first half of the nineteenth century it was possible for slaves in the Southern states to spend most of their stolen lives producing the cotton that stoked Britain's Industrial Revolution.

(Olusoga, 2016: 26)

It is now known that at a time when the importance of early childhood in the U.K. was seeing positive developments, we were also making iron slave collars to be used on children elsewhere in the world. Whilst not every philanthropist was involved in slavery, works such as *Britain's Forgotten Slave Owners* (BBC, 2015) or the Centre for the Study of the Legacies of British Slavery at University College London, are necessary commentaries into the way profit from the slave trade permeated (and therefore funded) all areas of life in Britain. For me, this brings into sharp relief why equality and diversity need to be such an integral part of our early childhood curriculum – for both practitioners and children. Discussions like this need to continue across the sector, so we can better understand our collective history. We need to learn more, we need to do more to acknowledge the past – so we can do better now, and in the future.

(Note: If this has raised questions for you, then I would urge you to explore the bibliography for more. In addition, my eternal thanks go to Dr Yinka Olusoga for help with this section to put some of the history into context.)

As we have explored, the history of the early childhood sector is a rich weaving together of ideas, thoughts, and opinions. Theorists and writers, academics and educators, philosophers and philanthropists who all believed in, and shared their values, beliefs, and observations on the importance of early childhood and play. People who took the metaphorical early childhood baton, studied it, added to it, analysed it, moulded it, developed it, and passed it on. We also have contemporary writers and thinkers, who continue to guide our reflections and practice. The works of Dr Jools Page (Professional Love), Prof. Chris Pascal and Prof. Tony Bertram (Centre for Research in Early Childhood [CREC]), and Dr Jack Shonkoff (Center on the Developing Child at Harvard) are amongst those who continue to advocate for the importance of early childhood. Today, we are ever grateful for those who passed on, and continue to pass on, the metaphorical baton of early childhood.

The observations, thoughts, knowledge and understanding of many have been carefully passed down the years to support our ongoing and developing knowledge of early childhood. This brief section begins to show how our understanding of play has been shaped and influenced. The names, many akin to old friends, are much cherished by those who continue to read, support, and share this work – and continue to pass on the baton to the new generation of early childhood practitioners. This *should* give us belief, a sense of security and a confidence in what we do. In addition, we can build on this "rootedness to our work" (Nutbrown and Clough, 2014: 3). We can add to the growing knowledge and understanding. We can consider how we pass the baton on.

This then leads to the questions:

How does this rich and vibrant history of the understanding of play link to our modern interpretations?
How can our ever-developing learning inform future practice?
How does this link to our understanding of neuroscience and brain development?

Our Understanding of Play

Our understanding of play comes from a range of places. As well as being influenced by the theory and research, some of which we have just explored, we have personal influences on our approaches to play. From before we are born, we are influenced by the things we hear, feel, and experience, and so on. You may have guessed from other chapters, or my other books or having heard me speak, that I am a huge advocate of the work of Urie

Bronfenbrenner (1917–2005), and that I have been greatly influenced by his work. There is one particular quote that is my all-time favourite, and one I use whenever possible:

> Learning and development are facilitated by the participation of the developing person in progressively more complex patterns of reciprocal activity with someone with whom that person has developed a strong and enduring emotional attachment and when the balance of power gradually shifts in favor of the developing person.
>
> (Bronfenbrenner, 1979: 60)

You probably hear this more often as the slightly misquoted, but easier to say and remember:

> In order to develop normally, a child requires progressively more complex joint activity with one or more adults … *Every child needs at least one adult who is irrationally crazy about him or her.*

Bronfenbrenner's ecological and bio-ecological models are well respected in the early childhood world, and definitely worth exploring (see bibliography). The original theory was specifically about the layers of influences on child development, and how they each interconnect. Later, Bronfenbrenner discussed how the systems could also be seen over a lifetime. Bronfenbrenner described the theory as "a set of nested structures, each inside the next, like a set of Russian dolls" (Bronfenbrenner, 1979: 22).

However, here we could also use Bronfenbrenner's ecological model as a way to explore our own understanding of play. We can consider our own experiences and interactions and explore how our thoughts and practices on play have been shaped and influenced:

Microsystem – Bronfenbrenner described the microsystem as the influences nearest to the developing child.
    In terms of exploring our approaches to play, this could be the influences from our own childhoods, our families, neighbourhoods, our cultures and so on.

In addition, there can be different microsystems that we move between. This could be, for example, our immediate close networks, such as college, university, workplace, colleagues, teams, leaders, and managers.

Mesosystem – Bronfenbrenner described the mesosystem as the way various microsystems interact with each other.

In terms of our approaches to play, this could be around if our childhood homes and schools agreed on play, or if there were conflicts. Did our neighbourhoods and communities support children to play or did they discourage it?

In addition, the mesosystem is about the various influences as we move between different microsystems. This, for example, could include the wide range of learning and work environments we move between. How do these influences link to our other microsystems – do they support? – or is there challenge or conflict?

Exosystem – Bronfenbrenner described the exosystem as systems that we are not directly involved in, but still have an influence.

In terms of our approaches to play, this could be media influences as well as local services, systems, politics, and policies on areas such as health, welfare, and education.

Macrosystem – Bronfenbrenner described the macrosystem as the impact from wider influences, such as a society's values, attitudes, beliefs, and assumptions. Overarching social, economic, political, health, education and legal systems also sit here.

If we consider historical perspectives again and think of Britain in the late 1800s–early 1900s as an example here, society believed children were not important. The phrase 'seen and not heard' is often used in association with this era, and clearly shows the culture, attitudes, and beliefs of the time. School attendance was not a legal requirement. Many children had to work to support their families, often in dangerous jobs in coal mines, factories, or cleaning chimneys. Access to healthcare was impossible for most ordinary families, and many children died from diseases such as measles, flu, and tuberculosis (TB, sometimes called consumption).

In terms of our approaches to play, this is about the society we live in now. What are the values, attitudes, beliefs, and assumptions today? What about the overarching systems? How do these things influence our approaches to play?

Chronosystem – Bronfenbrenner added the fifth system later and described the chronosystem as the influences over a period of time. Some influences remain constant and change very little, others can change dramatically. Changes can also be caused by events or experiences – and can be external/environmental or internal/personal. Changes can also be expected or unexpected. So, for example, starting a new school would be seen as external/environmental but expected, whereas a sudden serious illness would be internal/personal and not expected.

In terms of our approaches to play, this could include if we still feel the same about play as we did as children, or during initial learning, for example. How have key events or experiences influenced our approaches to play? What has changed over time, and why?

REFLECTIVE PRACTICE

Personal Influences on Play

Look back over the descriptions using Bronfenbrenner's model as a way to look at your influences on play.

Then, reconsider your thoughts from the earlier reflective practice exercise – 'What Is Play......?' at the beginning of this chapter. Then, consider the following questions:

Can you see where your influences have come from, and where they fit into the systems and layers?

Are there influences you had not considered earlier?

Has that changed your thinking? If so, how?

Can you see where the influences of your colleagues/teams/networks come from?

Can you see any challenges or conflicts?

Why do you think that is?

Any other thoughts?

I am sure that your reflections will clearly show how we all have our own unique systems, and how as we move around, we interact with other people, and *their* unique systems. Our influences may be similar, or completely different, or perhaps even challenging or conflicting. Therefore, our approaches to play may be similar, completely different, or perhaps even challenging or conflicting. The key here is how we, as a sector, create a true and honest "community of practice" (Lave and Wenger, 1991; Wenger, 1998) that continues to strive to recognise, acknowledge and promote the value of play.

> As you are reading this ... I encourage you to think about the communities you are part of, what you might do for them, and how they benefit your work.
>
> (Murray, 2019: 116)

In other words, how do we use the various systems and communities we are part of to best support early childhood? How do we take all of our previous influences, personal, environmental, expected, and unexpected, and build on the rich evidence-based, research-informed history of the importance of play in early childhood? How can we help and support other systems that maybe do not always understand our philosophies? How do we create a unified and comprehensive approach to play?

And importantly, where does that leave us now? The theorists passed on the metaphorical 'play baton' and charged us with ensuring that play remains central to childhood. How do we pass the baton on? Is there a baton to pass on – is it in danger of being lost?

When *this* book is published, the early childhood world will be able to refer to over 2000 years of evidence-based, research-informed practice and theory, as we have seen, from a range of sources. In relation to early development, play features highly throughout. Yet, it appears that, even now, there are areas where the importance, impact and criticality of play is still mocked, misunderstood, or misinterpreted – areas where the importance of play still has to be defended. Maybe it is about time we reclaimed our history and our heritage in discussions around future developments regarding the importance of, and understanding of, early childhood and play:

> [This] sometimes stems from poor interpretations of principles of good practice, such as when "developmentally appropriate practice" is taken to mean

that teachers let children play aimlessly or leave them to '"develop" totally on their own (Kostelnik, 1992). At other times, it may stem from the thinking lodged in the day care versus education dichotomy... we are still struggling with the value of [early childhood].

(Phillips and Bredekamp, 1998: 444)

As Daniel (2018: 5) discusses:

In an ideal situation Members of Parliament, Theorists, Economists, Educators, Parents, and the society at large would have a universally agreed value system for the EYS [Early Years Sector] which would in turn ensure a consistent approach that would be sustainable beyond the political party that is in power. However, the current EYS is afflicted with the undue burden of rapid and relentless change and the opinionated vagaries of opposing political parties. These dynamics, alongside rolling policy development, continue apace to shape (or misshape) the EYS.

REFLECTIVE PRACTICE

Passing on the Baton for Play?

Let's take a moment to reflect on where we feel we are currently, in terms of our approaches to play. Think about the following quotes:
Frost, (1998: 8) offers:

Play is essential for healthy development as it seems to facilitate the linkages of language, emotion, movement, socialisation, and cognition. It is playful activity ... that makes a positive difference in brain development and human functioning.

Lillard et al. (2013: 28) discuss:

The hands-on, child driven educational methods sometimes referred to as "playful learning" (Hirsh-Pasek et al., 2009) are the most positive means yet known to help young children's development.

Drew (2019: 216) states:

There remains the likelihood that children's play spaces and play activities will continue to be restricted and restructured to meet the anxieties of adults, rather than the needs or desires of children.

Then consider the following questions:

How do you feel reading the quotes?
How do the quotes relate to your beliefs, values and understanding of play?
How do the quotes relate to your practice, beliefs, and your influences:
To your colleagues/teams?
To your workplace?
Does local and national policy support your practice to support and develop children's play?
Why do you feel that?
How do you think we can ensure we have a baton to pass on to future play and early childhood practitioners?
Why do you think that?
Any other thoughts?

However we feel about the current outlook on play, we need to ensure we build on our rich history, add to the knowledge, and work out a way to pass this forward. I would like to go back to the historical theorists' grid and give the final word in this section to Huizinga (1955: 1094).

> Whatever happens, whatever we believe, (now or in the future), play should never be "to order."

The Case for Early Childhood: The Case for Play

So, I think we have now come full circle, well almost. I think it is safe to say that play matters! We can utilise our rich and diverse history to share the evidence for play and child development and why we should value childhood. In addition, there is evidence that, economically, investing in early childhood resources makes a bigger impact on long-term economic developments. Art Rolnick and Rob Grunewald (2003) of the Minneapolis Federal Reserve Bank found that:

> Early education investments yield a return that far exceeds the return on most public projects that are considered economic development…yielding more than $8 for every $1 invested.
>
> (Clothier and Poppe, 2004 [no page])

Furthermore, Nobel Prize–winning University of Chicago Economics Professor James Heckman has spent a lifetime researching the impacts of early childhood. (The Heckman Equation website has a wealth of easily accessible materials, many of which are free to use and share, and I would urge you to explore this further.) As Heckman and Masterov (2007: 24) explain:

> Early skills breed later skills because early learning begets [causes] later learning. … investment in the young is warranted. Returns are highest for investments made at younger ages and remedial investments are often prohibitively costly. … Returns for disadvantaged children are highest for investments made at young ages.

In other words, it makes sense to invest in early childhood, as it costs much more to put things 'right' later. Art Rolnick, James Heckman and others may be talking about the impact of economic investment in support of early childhood, and I recognise this can be seen to be purely about money. However, the case for investment in early childhood is also clear in relation to the impact on brain development.

> A fundamental paradox exists and is unavoidable: development in the early years is both highly robust and highly vulnerable. Although there have been long-standing debates about how much the early years really matter in the larger scheme of lifelong development, our conclusion is unequivocal: What happens during the first months and years of life matters a lot, not because this period of development provides an indelible blueprint for adult well-being, but because it sets either a sturdy or fragile stage for what follows.
>
> (Shonkoff and Phillips, 2000: 5)

In other words, development in early childhood matters as it paves the way for what follows, be it sturdy or fragile. So, does this include play? Does play support brain development? Well, it turns out that science can answer that question too:

> Did you know that the most important interactions you have with a child can happen through play? By engaging in playful serve and return with a child, you can literally help build stronger connections in the brain. Strong neural connections are the foundation for all of a child's future learning, behavior, and health.
>
> (Center on the Developing Child, 2022)

Or, to put it another way, those simple, early childhood classics of back-and-forth, give-and-take, synchronised interactions. In other words – play! From repeating baby's babbling noises and playing peek-a-boo, to rolling a ball, the uncomplicated but vital exchanges between a child and an in-tune adult (and we will explore this more later). The biological evidence for this is growing and deepening. For example, research is now showing children who experience consistent 'serve and return' relationships have greater brain volume (especially grey matter), better language development, lower stress levels and better development of empathy. And, due to ongoing scientific development we can actually see photographs and images of how this looks and works. (See bibliography for more.)

I am sure it will come as no surprise that there is always going to be some grey areas when it comes to brain development and the ongoing advances in neuroscience. For example, this rather lovely quote regularly does the rounds on social media, purportedly said by the late Dr Karyn Purvis, a researcher and developmental psychologist; however, nowhere can I find any substantiated source.

> Scientists have recently determined that it takes approximately 400 repetitions to create a new synapse in the brain—unless it is done with play, in which case, it takes between 10 and 20 repetitions!
>
> Dr. Karyn Purvis

Wouldn't that be a lovely thought – that play makes connections faster in the brain. So, although I cannot find any confirmed basis for this particular quote, Dr Purvis was a highly regarded academic and it is easy to find her work if you wanted to explore it further. (Oh, and if you do find the origin of the quote, please do let me know.) What we *can* prove, however, is that a developing brain forms more than 1 million new neural connections every second. I think that is phenomenal. This is why I love what I do, and why I am so passionate about the early childhood sector...because what we do for every child, literally every second of every day, helps.

There is a link with sustained shared thinking here too, where an in-tune adult supports and encourages a child to develop their thinking and learning, through carefully supported play. Like serve and return – there is a back and forth here too that supports the developing brain to make connections through play. Sustained shared thinking is a finely tuned balance between the child and adult leading, which questions, clarifies, develops, and extends ideas and thinking (Brodie, 2009: 2014). Like this case study from Carey, which looks at the way serve and return, and sustained shared thinking, support a child to develop neural connections as their thinking and learning develops. Carey is a practitioner who works in a preschool setting; Shaykh is 4 years old and has been at the setting for some time. This is Shaykh's last term before going to school. Carey discusses an interaction with Shaykh:

Sticky Tape Fingerprints

Shaykh is in the craft area and engaged in sticking bottle tops onto a piece of paper, skilfully using the sticky tape dispenser. As Shaykh pulls a piece of tape off the dispenser, Shaykh notices a fingerprint on the clear tape.

"I can see my fingerprint!" Shaykh commented to me.

"Oh yes! Did the police talk to you about fingerprints when they came to visit nursery?" I asked.

"No, but I've seen it on my television before", Shaykh explained. "Someone's lunch had been stolen and they used fingerprints to catch the person that took it."

"It's a bit hard to see the prints", commented Shaykh. I suggested that we could stick the tape onto some coloured paper so they could try and see the fingerprints a bit clearer. Shaykh found some coloured paper and returned to the table to stick the tape onto the paper.

We worked together to help each other collect fingerprints from our fingers, talking about which finger was next and who had the biggest fingers.

Shaykh said, "It's a bit difficult to see the prints" and together we thought about why they were still a bit blurry.

"Perhaps we have to do it really slowly and carefully, so the print stays on the tape", suggested Shaykh. This seemed to work and create clearer marks.

Together, we looked closely at the marks and discussed the patterns we could see.

"Did you know that your fingerprint is unique to you? Only you have those patterns, which is why the police can see who they belong to if they need to", I asked.

"Yes, they said that on my television!" replied Shaykh.

The interaction then came to a natural end.

Fingerprints were not the planned objective for this lovely example of interaction and sustained shared thinking. The activity was truly child-led, as it came purely from the child's interest.

Reflections on how this could be extended for the child:

- Use ink pads to create fingerprints.
- Revisit the TV cartoon to see what information could be used or extended.
- Use mathematical language to describe the size and shape of the prints.
- Use descriptive language to describe the patterns.
- Find magnifying glasses to examine the prints.
- Photocopy/enlarge the prints from the child and the practitioner so you can clearly see the differences in the patterns.

This activity became a teachable moment by careful scaffolding from Carey, a highly skilled, in-tune and interested practitioner. Talking about prior experience (the recent visit from the police) prompted and empowered Shaykh to be able to relate it to prior knowledge (the TV cartoon). Working together (back and forth/serve and return) they were able to resolve the problems they encountered (not being able to see the prints clearly). All of which will have supported neural connections in Shaykh's brain. A true sustained shared thinking, learning moment... but I bet Shaykh wouldn't call it that.

Therefore, to bring all of this together:

Research can evidence how 'serve and return' type activities strengthen neural connections and support brain development.

Evidence shows that early childhood investment makes a difference, and financially costs less in the longer term.

Science shows us that the developing brain is pre-programmed to respond to environments and what is happening around it (whether useful, stressful, or otherwise).

Over 2000 years of evidenced-based, research-informed early childhood theory and practice is available to build on.

There are laws that advocate the 'right to play' (UNCRC, 1989).

So back to the discussions at the beginning of this chapter:

> Play Matters.... This is a book about neuroscience and the science behind brain development. Can the two *really* go together? Can science *really* help us to understand why play matters? Are there areas other than early childhood where we can look for evidence?

I will leave you to reflect on those questions and consider how the discussions we have explored in this chapter might help you in your practice and might help the early childhood community to pass on the baton to future practitioners. After all, as we have explored many times, it is adults who have the biggest influence on childhood and brain development – and we will explore more of that in a later chapter.

And finally, just a couple of quotes, to bring this chapter to a close:

> Children can and will play in most places. A rich environment for play includes: natural elements; opportunities for risk and challenge; places to express emotions; stimulation for the senses; chances for social interactions; interesting and varied physical and human environments and sufficient space to do what is wanted.
>
> (International Play Association, 2014)

Children have a built-in, innate ability to play: a small puddle, a blowing leaf, or a few pebbles can create hours of fun. Yes, there is probably learning, but whether the children would call it that is another matter. I would like the final words on play to go to folklorists Peter and Iona Opie. The Opies dedicated their lives to studying childhood culture, children at play, and the history of classic childhood games and rhymes. Their books have been a constant friend and companion throughout my career. This is from "Street Games: Counting-Out and Chasing" (1969: 638):

> Where children are, is where they play.

Chapter Reflection

Thinking back over this chapter, consider the various elements (sections, quotes, reflective exercises, terminology, etc.). Are there any elements that:

Were particularly useful?
Need re-reading, or more thought or reflection?
You want to look up and/or explore further?

Any other thoughts or reflections?

Bibliography

The following are books, articles, web pages, organisations, documents, etc. that I have found useful (online versions, all accessed 20 July 2022). Some are directly referenced in this chapter – some are included as valuable sources of background reading that might be helpful. See also web resources at the end of Chapter 1.

Ardley, G. (1967) The role of play in the philosophy of Plato. *Philosophy*, 42(161), pp. 226–244.

Balgarnie, R. (1878) *Sir Titus Salt, Baronet: His Life and its Lessons*. London: Hodder and Stoughton.

Besio, S. (2018) Play for the sake of play: in pursuit of a dream? In: S. Besio and T. Zappaterra, eds. *Children's Play: Multifaceted Aspects* (Vol. 13). ETS. Florence: University of Bergamo, pp. 43–70.

Britain's Forgotten Slave Owners; Episode 1 - Profit and Loss [television programme] BBC, U.K., 15 July 2015. Directed by James Van Der Pool. BBC iPlayer, 59 mins. Available at: https://www.bbc.co.uk/iplayer/episode/b062nqpd/britains-forgotten-slave-owners-1-profit-and-loss [Accessed 07 March 2022].

Britain's Forgotten Slave Owners; Episode 2 - The Price of Freedom [television programme] BBC, U.K., 15 July 2015. Directed by James Van Der Pool. BBC iPlayer, 59 mins. Available at: https://www.bbc .co.uk/iplayer/episode/b063jzdw/britains-forgotten-slave-owners-2 -the-price-of-freedom [Accessed 07 March 2022].

Brodie, K. (2009) *Sustained Shared Thinking: How Important is it?* [blog] 02 February. Available at: www.kathybrodie.com/viewpoint /sustained-shared-thinking-important.

Brodie, K. (2014) *Sustained Shared Thinking in the Early Years: Linking Theory to Practice.* Abingdon: Routledge.

Bronfenbrenner, U. (1979) *The Ecology of Human Development: Experiments by Nature and Design.* Cambridge, MA: Harvard University Press.

Bronfenbrenner, U. (1986) Ecology of the family as a context for human development. *Developmental Psychology,* 22(6), pp. 723–742. Available at: https://psycnet.apa.org/doi/10.1037/0012-1649.22.6.723.

Bronfenbrenner, U. (1992) *Ecological Systems Theory.* London: Jessica Kingsley Publishers.

Bronfenbrenner, U. and Ceci, S. J. (1994) Nature-nurture reconceptualized in developmental perspective: a bioecological model. *Psychological Review,* 101, pp. 568–586. Available at: https://doi.org/10.1037/0033-295x.101.4.568.

Bruner, J. S. (1972) Nature and uses of immaturity. In: P. K. Smith and A. D. Pellegrini, eds. *Psychology of Education: Pupils and Learning* (Vol. 2). London: Taylor and Francis, pp. 52–88.

Centre for the Study of the Legacies of British Slavery. (2022). Available at: https://www.ucl.ac.uk/lbs/.

Clothier, S. and Poppe, J. (2004) National conference of state legislatures. *New Research: Early Education as Economic Investment.* [blog] 10 September. Available at: https://www.ncsl.org/blog/2014/09/10/early -learning-fellows-hear-benefits-of-early-childhood-investment.aspx.

Colliver, Y. and Doel-Mackaway, H. (2021) Article 31, 31 years on: choice and autonomy as a framework for implementing children's right to play in early childhood services. *Human Rights Law Review*, 21(3), pp. 566–587. Available at: https://doi.org/10.1093/hrlr/ngab011.

Convention on the rights of the child. (1989) Treaty no. 27531. *United Nations Treaty Series*, 1577, pp. 3–178.

D'Angour, A. (2013) Plato and play: taking education seriously in ancient Greece. *American Journal of Play*, 5(3), pp. 293–307. Available at: https://files.eric.ed.gov/fulltext/EJ1016076.pdf.

Daniel, V. (2018) *Perceptions of a Leadership Crisis in the Early Years Sector (EYS)*. EdD Thesis. Birmingham: University of Birmingham. Available at: https://etheses.bham.ac.uk//id/eprint/8787/1/Daniel2019EdD.pdf.

Drew, C. (2019) We call this "play", however…: navigating 'play anxiety' in early childhood education and care markets. *Journal of Early Childhood Research*, 17(2), pp. 116–128. Available at: https://doi.org/10.1177%2F1476718X18809385.

Fonseca-Azevedo, K. and Herculano-Houzel, S. (2012) Metabolic constraint imposes tradeoff between body size and number of brain neurons in human evolution. *Proceedings of the National Academy of Sciences*, 109(45), pp. 18571–18576. Available at: https://doi.org/10.1073/pnas.1206390109.

Froebel, F. (1887) *The Education of Man* (W. N. Hailman Trans). New York: Appleton and Co. Ltd. (*Original work published in 1906*).

Frost, J. L. (1998) *Neuroscience, Play and Child Development*. Paper presented by the IPA/USA Triennial National Conference. [ERIC Document 427 845, PS 027 328.].

Heckman, J. J. and Masterov, D. V. (2007) *The Productivity Argument for Investing in Young Children*. Cambridge, MA: National Bureau of Economic Research. Available at: https://jenni.uchicago.edu/papers/Heckman_Masterov_RAE_2007_v29_n3.pdf.

See also: Heckman Equation. Available at: https://heckmanequation.org/

Herculano-Houzel, S. (2016) *The Human Advantage: A New Understanding of How Our Brain Became Remarkable.* Cambridge, MA: MIT Press.

Hirsh-Pasek, K., Golinkoff, R., Berk, L. and Singer, D. (2009) *A Mandate for Playful Learning in Preschool: Presenting the Evidence.* New York: Oxford University Press.

International Play Association (IPA) (2014) *Declaration on Play.* Available at: http://ipaworld.org/wp-content/uploads/2015/05/IPA_Declaration-FINAL.pdf.

Isaacs, S. (1948) *Childhood and After: Some Essays and Clinical Studies.* London: Routledge and Kegan Paul. In: R. Parker-Rees and J. Willan, eds. (2006). *Early Years Education: Histories and Traditions* (Vol. 1). London: Taylor and Francis.

Isaacs, S. (1951 edition) *Social Development in Young Children.* London: Routledge.

Kennedy, C. (2000) *Business Pioneers: Family, Fortune, and Philanthropy: Cadbury, Sainsbury and John Lewis.* London: Random House Business Books.

Krentz, A. A. (1998) Play and education in Plato's republic. *The Paideia Archive: Twentieth World Congress of Philosophy,* 29, pp. 199–207. Available at: https://doi.org/10.5840/wcp20-paideia199829497.

Kostelnik, M. J. (1992) Myths associated with developmentally appropriate programs. *Young Children,* 47(4), pp. 17–23.

Kuzawa, C. W., Chugani, H. T., Grossman, L. I., Lipovich, L., Muzik, O., Hof, P. R., Wildman, D. E., Sherwood, C. C., Leonard, W. R. and Lange, N., (2014) Metabolic costs and evolutionary implications of human brain development. *Proceedings of the National Academy of Sciences,* 111(36), pp. 13010–13015. Available at: https://doi.org/10.1073/pnas.1323099111.

Lave, J. and Wenger, E. (1991) *Situated Learning: Legitimate Peripheral Participation.* Cambridge: Cambridge University Press.

Lillard, A. S., Lerner, M. D., Hopkins, E. J., Dore, R. A., Smith, E. D., and Palmquist, C. (2013) The impact of pretend play on children's development: a review of the evidence. *Psychological Bulletin*, 139(1), pp. 1–34. Available at: https://doi.org/10.1037/a0029321.

Montessori, M. (1912) *The Montessori Method: Scientific Pedagogy as Applied to Child Education in 'the Children's Houses' with Additions and Revisions by the Author* (A. E. George, Trans.). Cambridge, MA: Robert Bentley.

Montessori, M. (1949) *The Absorbent Mind.* Adyar: The Theosophical Publishing House.

Murray, J. (2019) Our community in early years education. *International Journal of Early Years Education*, 27(2), pp. 115–117. Available at: https://doi.org/10.1080/09669760.2019.1606766.

Nutbrown, C. and Clough, P. (2014) *Early Childhood Education: History, Philosophy and Experience.* London: Sage.

OECD (Organisation for Economic Co-operation and Development) (2002) *Understanding the Brain: Towards a New Learning Science.* Paris: OECD Publishing.

Olusoga, D. (2016) *Black and British: A Forgotten History.* London: Macmillan.

Owen, R. D. (1814) *A New View of Society: Or Essays on the Principle of the Formation of the Human Character, and the Application of the Principle to Practice: Essay 3* (Vol. 3). London: R and A Taylor.

Owen, R. D. (1824) *An Outline of the System of Education at New Lanark.* Printed at the University Press, for Wardlaw and Cunninghame.

Owen. R. D. (1842) *The Book of the New Moral World: Containing the Rational System of Society, Founded on Demonstrable Facts, Developing the Constitution and Laws of Human Nature and of Society.* New York: G. Vale.

Pascal, C. and Bertram, T. (2016) *High Achieving White Working Class (HAWWC) Boys Project: Final Report.* Birmingham: CREC (Centre for Research in Early Childhood). Available at: https://www.crec.co.uk/hawwc-boys.

Page, J. (2011) Do mothers want professional carers to love their babies? *Journal of Early Childhood Research*, 9(3), pp. 310–323. Available at: https://doi.org/10.1177%2F1476718X11407980.

Page, J. (2014) Developing professional love in early childhood settings. In: L. Harrison and J. Sumsion, eds. *International Perspectives on Early Childhood and Development: Lived Spaces of Infant-Toddler Education and Care: Exploring Diverse Perspectives on Theory, Research and Practice*. Dordrecht, NL: Springer, pp. 119–130.

Page, J. (2016) Educators' perspectives on attachment and professional love in early years settings in England. In: E. J. White and C. Dalli, eds. *Under Three-Year-Olds in Policy and Practice: Policy and Pedagogy with Under-Three-Year-Olds: Cross-Disciplinary Insights and Innovations for Educational Research with Very Young Children Series*. Dordrecht, NL: Springer, pp. 131–142.

Page, J. (2017) Reframing Infant-Toddler pedagogy through a lens of professional love: exploring narratives of professional practice in early childhood settings in England. *Contemporary Issues in Early Childhood*, 18(4), pp. 387–399. Available at: https://doi.org/10.1177%2F1463949117742780.

Shonkoff, J. P. and Phillips, D. A., eds. (2000) *From Neurons to Neighborhoods: The Science of Early Childhood Development*. Washington, DC: National Academy Press.

Phillips, C. B. and Bredekamp, S. (1998) Reconsidering Early Childhood Education. In: C. P. Edwards, L. Gandini and G. E. Forman, eds. *The Hundred Languages of Children: The Reggio Emilia Approach–Advanced Reflections*. Greenwich, CT: Ablex Publishing Corporation.

Purves, Karyn Dr. - More information. Available at: https://child.tcu.edu/#sthash.B22JxS7B.dpbs.

Quintilian (1963) *Institutio Oratoria, Vol 1*. Translated by H. E. Butler. Cambridge, MA: Harvard University Press.

Rolnick, A. J. and Grunewald, R. (2003) Early childhood development: Economic development with a high public return. [blog] *Federal Reserve Bank of Minneapolis*, 1 March. Available at: https://www

.minneapolisfed.org/article/2003/early-childhood-development -economic-development-with-a-high-public-return.

Rowlatt, J. and Knight, L. (2021) The real reason humans are the dominant species. *BBC News*, 28 March. Available at: https://www .bbc.co.uk/news/science-environment-56544239.

Ryall, E., Russell, W. and MacLean, M., eds. (2013) *The Philosophy of Play*. Abingdon: Routledge.

Shonkoff (2009) Mobilizing science to revitalize early childhood policy. *Issues in Science and Technology*, 26(1), pp. 79–85. Available at: https://www.jstor.org/stable/43315005.

Shonkoff, J. P. and Phillips, D. A., eds. (2000) *From Neurons to Neighborhoods: The Science of Early Childhood Development*. Washington, DC: National Academy Press.

Wenger, E. (1998) *Communities of Practice: Learning, Meaning, and Identity*. New York: Cambridge University Press.

Worthington, E. (1889) *Jean Jacques Rousseau: Emile; Or Concerning Education*. Boston: D.C. Heath and Co.

The following can all be found in:

Bruner, J. S., Jolly, A. and Sylva, K., eds. (2017) *Play its Role in Development and Evolution*. New York: Basic Books. (Available as: e-Book 2017 International Psychotherapy Institute). Available at: https://www.researchgate.net/publication/328486788_Play_its _role_in_development_and_evolution.

Dolinhow, P. (1971) At play in the fields. (From a Special Supplement of the Natural History Magazine, December 1971). In: J. S. Bruner, A. Jolly and K. Sylva, eds. *Play Its Role in Development and Evolution*. New York: Basic Books. (Available as: e-Book 2017 International Psychotherapy Institute).

Huizinga, J. (1955) Play and contest as civilizing functions (From Homo Ludens: A Study of the Play Element in Culture, The Beacon Press, Boston, U.S.A., 1955 [first published in 1939]). In: J. S. Bruner, A. Jolly and K. Sylva, eds. *Play Its Role in Development and Evolution.* New York: Basic Books. (Available as: e-Book 2017 International Psychotherapy Institute).

Opie, I. and Opie, P. (1969) Street games: Counting-out and chasing. (From Children's Games in Street and Playground, Clarendon Press). In: J. S. Bruner, A. Jolly and K. Sylva, eds. *Play Its Role in Development and Evolution.* New York: Basic Books. (Available as: e-Book 2017 International Psychotherapy Institute).

Vygotsky, L. (1933) Play and its role in the mental development of the child. (From Soviet Psychology, Vol. 12, No. 6, 1966, pp. 62–76. The article was transcribed from a stenographic record of a lecture given in 1933 at the Hertzen Pedagogical Institute, Leningrad). In: J. S. Bruner, A. Jolly and K. Sylva, eds. *Play Its Role in Development and Evolution.* New York: Basic Books. (Available as: e-Book 2017 International Psychotherapy Institute).

As we have explored elsewhere, human babies arrive in the world wholly reliant on others. This includes parents, grandparents, aunties and uncles, neighbours and friends, communities and professionals, societies, and governments. We have looked at how environments (both the physical and emotional) have a crucial role. We have considered over 2000 years of child development–focused evidence. We have explored some of the science behind brain development. And, we have considered how we could perhaps look to other sectors and disciplines for ideas, such as ethnography.

Throughout all of this exploration, there has been one critical theme. You (or me) or us – adults!

As adults, in whatever role (or roles) we find ourselves, we have a vital part to play in supporting child development, and therefore brain development. Neuroscience now has growing evidence that the warm, secure, reciprocal, consistent and loving interactions, connections, and relationships we form with children are the basis of healthy brain development (Page, 2014, 2017; Pascal and Bertram, 2016; Harvard Center on the Developing Child, 2022).

In order to understand the role of adults in supporting brain development, there are some key terms we need to explore. Whilst these terms are crucially important and could easily have a whole chapter or book each, these are just some very brief and basic descriptions for some context. This book is an introduction to neuroscience, and I would urge you to consider the bibliography for some excellent places to explore these topics in greater depth.

DOI: 10.4324/9781003154846-5

Key Brain Development Terms

Brain Architecture
Serve and Return
Self-Regulation
Executive Function
Resilience
Toxic Stress

Brain Architecture

Architecture simply means building. Experiences from before conception affect the physical development of the brain. Nurturing and supportive environments and experiences, including healthy lifestyles, and consistent, warm, loving, positive relationships help to build a strong foundation for healthy brain development.

Serve and Return

As we mentioned in Chapter 4, 'serve and return' is the term for the hundreds (if not thousands) of back-and-forth interactions that happen every day. These include eye contact, facial expressions, gestures, gentle touch, cuddles and hugs, talking and singing, and so on.

Self-Regulation

Regulation means control, manage or use. So self-regulation is the ability to control, manage and use our own (self) emotions and behaviours. In addition, self-regulation involves being able to control our own thoughts. Self-regulation is interwoven with executive function. (See also Chapter 6).

Executive Function

Executive means managing and function means task – so executive function literally means managing tasks. Executive function is about memory, planning, and managing lots of information at the same time, for example.

Resilience

Resilience means flexibility, strength, adaptability, etc. Resilience is about being able to be flexible and adaptable. Resilience also includes the ability (and/or strength) to cope with things such as uncertainty, change, setbacks, disruptions, challenges, and difficulties.

Toxic Stress

As we discussed in Chapter 1, toxic stress is stress that is regular and/or persistent, and prolonged over a period of time – and where there is no support available to cushion or buffer the stress.

Together, these key terms give us a simple blueprint of what brains need (and do not need) in order to develop and learn, flourish, and thrive. All of these key terms rely on the support of trusted, consistent, loving relationships. (See web resources at the end of Chapter 1 for more.) Let's explore this a little further.

REFLECTIVE PRACTICE

Exploring Key Brain Development Terms

Think about the last time you tried to learn a new skill – where you needed support from a teacher/professional/tutor, etc. This could be anything, a new craft, playing an instrument, learning a language maybe, or learning to drive, for example.

Now consider the key brain development terms.

Brain Architecture
What did you need from the adults around you?
(At home and where the learning took place?)
Serve and Return
What helped you to progress, develop and learn?
(At home and where the learning took place?)
Self-Regulation
As you learnt, what helped you to cope with the things you found difficult?
(At home and where the learning took place?)
Executive Function
What helped you to be able to concentrate?
(At home and where the learning took place?)
Resilience
What helped you to continue with the learning, even when things were difficult?
(At home and where the learning took place?)

Now consider that life is not always as easy as you'd like.
Toxic Stress
What help would you need for stress to be positive (to help you to concentrate, etc.), or tolerable and temporary?
(At home and where the learning is to take place?)

Anything else you want to add?

There are times when all our brains need support to function and develop. I am sure from your reflections that you are able to pinpoint the environments and relationships that supported your developing brain architecture. You will be able to remember those moments that helped (or didn't) – the eye contact, facial expressions, the language used, and so on.

When you found things difficult, stressful, or frustrating, did you have someone who helped you to rebalance, and bring your emotions and feelings under control? This is known as co-regulation (see Chapter 6). Even as adults, when we are upset, angry, frustrated, over-excited, etc., we may need someone to help us regulate our emotions. Co-regulation includes the other person recognising and acknowledging the emotions we are experiencing. This validates our personal experiences. I am sure you have memories of experiencing intense emotions and being told to simply 'calm down'. I am also sure you can recall how that made you feel? Being told to 'calm down' dismisses our emotions and feelings and tells us they are not important.

Furthermore, if you requested help with your learning, did you know that the teacher/tutor would come to you, or did you feel abandoned and left to struggle? How did you feel?

Being able to self-regulate develops from supportive relationships and environments of co-regulation. Shonkoff and Phillips (2000: 121) offer:

> Stated simply, early development [of self-regulation] entails the gradual transition from extreme dependency on others to manage the world for us, to acquiring the competencies needed to manage the world for oneself.

If we are supported to self-regulate our feelings and emotions, we can then regulate our thinking and behaviours (see also Chapter 6). If you think back to learning your new skill, you needed to use your executive functioning skills. Using memories of previous or similar experiences helps to consolidate new learning (and build neural pathways and connections). Did you manage to ignore the birds flying around outside, the drilling in another part of the building, the traffic going past, thinking about what to cook for dinner, or the email you need to send later? All while listening to the instructions from the tutor/teacher. Executive functioning is often talked of as similar to air traffic control – so trying to manage lots of planes (thoughts) flying around at the same time and making sure they all go where they are supposed to, and at the right time.

In addition, could you wait for certain things? If you were desperate to go and meet a friend, for example, could you wait, at least for a little while? This is known as delaying gratification and is linked to self-regulation, and helps to explain why self-regulation is sometimes called effortful control. This is also associated with being able to resist risky and impulsive behaviours.

Did you show resilience in your learning? Did you persevere, even when things were difficult? Did you bounce back after a problem or a setback? Could you still undertake your learning, even if things in your life were difficult elsewhere? Did the environment and relationships support you with this?

Or did the environment and relationships – both at home and where the learning took place – not help with your learning and development and so tip your stress levels from positive or tolerable into toxic? (See Chapter 1 for more.)

I am sure you can see where this is going. If this is what it feels like for adults, then how does it feel for children? The skills needed to cope in everyday life, such as being able to avoid distractions, concentrate, being able to take turns, being able to cope with change and being flexible, etc., take time to develop. Children are not born with these skills. At times, we all need support – and environments and relationships are central to how we perceive that support. Relationships and environments play a crucial part in the development of these skills – or not, as the case may be. As adults (mostly) create and control the environments that children find themselves in, and adults are key in the relationships in children's lives, then adults are critical to developing brain architecture. (See Chapters 2 and 6 for more.)

The Role of the Adult as a Brain Builder

The term 'Brain Builders' has been around for some time, and it is difficult to find its origins. 'Brain builders' is used in all manner of books, games, and puzzles, advertised as being designed to support children and adults with thinking, logic, and attention skills. 'Brain builders' is also used for products and services associated with memory loss. From our point of view, 'brain builders' is often used as a metaphor for the role we as adults play in supporting brain development. Just like the foundations of a house need to be strong, the developing brain needs strong foundations to grow and develop – and that is where we, as adults, come in. (See bibliography at the end of Chapter 1 for a host of resources, many of which are free to access and share.)

Brain development is referred to as being built from the bottom up – so from the brain stem upwards. However, in everyday life, the brain needs several of its areas to work together all at the same time, including the ones that could be furthest apart. As we mentioned in chapter Chapter 1, messages come into the brain via the central nervous system and arrive at the base of the brain first, before travelling upwards. Once a message is received, the brain then has to work out where to send the message, and how to respond. If the same messages are received over and over and over, the circuits and connections strengthen and develop over time. For developing brains, this takes time, and requires practice (a lot of practice). In order for the brain to learn how all the different sections work together, several things have to happen first – and they all rely on adults.

In Chapter 2, we briefly considered the critical work of Bronfenbrenner; now let's explore it in a little more depth. Urie Bronfenbrenner (1917–2005) was a Russian-born American psychologist, known for his influential work studying child development (see bibliography for more). Usually, Bronfenbrenner's ecological model is shown as a set of circles, with the child at the centre, with each circle getting bigger and moving outwards from the centre, a bit like onion rings. (A quick Google search will bring up some useful articles and diagrams if you want to explore this further.)

As we discussed earlier, Bronfenbrenner (1979: 22) uses the term of 'a nested Russian doll' system approach. In other words, the systems, or levels, of the model 'nest' inside one another. I think the term 'nested' works particularly well as it means snuggled, cuddled, and pull close – and the idea of 'systems' of support pulling closely together to support the child at the centre is one I think we can all identify with. In the original model there are four systems. Bronfenbrenner explored how the four interact to support the 'developing person' (or child) at the centre. As we considered in the earlier chapter, the model can be used to reflect on our own systems, with us at the centre, and how the various systems influence us. In fact, Bronfenbrenner often talked about 'across the lifespan', and the model could be used at any stage in life to consider the various influences. For the purposes of this chapter though, let's explore Bronfenbrenner's model to concentrate on children, and specifically in relation to brain development – and the role of the adult.

The 'ecological model' has evolved, developed, and been adapted to become one of the key child development theories. There are many versions and variations of the model available; for me though, it is always helpful to consider the terminology first, and then consider what that might mean. The following, therefore, is an exploration of the ecological model in words, rather than as the more usual diagram of circles.

An Exploration of the Ecological Model (adapted from Bronfenbrenner)

Name of System	Explanation	Description
Microsystem	Micro – means small or small scale. In the ecological model this means nearest or closest to the child at the centre.	This is defined as the immediate surroundings, and how they are experienced. Home, family, childcare, school, and friendships, for example, are all versions of a microsystem.
Mesosystem	Meso – means middle or intermediate (between two things).	The mesosystem is the interactions between the various systems. This includes the interactions between parents, practitioners and settings or school, for example.
Exosystem	Exo – means external, outer or from the outside.	The exosystem are systems that have an influence on what happens to the child but the child is not involved directly. For example, this could include extended families, communities, the parents' workplaces, governments, media, services.
Macrosystem	Macro – means large scale, overall.	The macrosystem includes national and global influences from social and cultural values and beliefs, war, economics, environment, etc.

Later, Bronfenbrenner added a fifth system, known as the 'chronosystem':

Name of System	Explanation	Description
Chronosystem	Chronos – from the Greek word, meaning time.	The chronosystem considers how the other systems change, interact, and develop over time.

For now, let's explore what this might mean in terms of neuroscience.

REFLECTIVE PRACTICE
Ecological Model Influences on Brain Development

Consider the systems within Bronfenbrenner's ecological model. Can you think of ways that each of the systems potentially influences children and the developing brain?

There are a couple of examples included to help. There are no right/wrong answers, as each child will be developing within their own unique systems, and you may well be thinking about specific children as you reflect on this.

(You could also refer back to your reflections on *your* influences within the ecological model in the chapter on play if that would be helpful.)

System	Potential Influences?
Microsystem (closest to the child)	• Parental health and wellbeing • Staff turnover at setting/school
Mesosystem (interactions between systems)	• Parent/practitioner partnerships • Connections within communities

Exosystem (outside influences)	• Uncertain work environment • Availability of services
Macrosystem (overall influences)	• Beliefs on discipline • Approaches to sleep routines
Chronosystem (time)	• Downturn in family finances • Long-term illness (child or family)

Using Bronfenbrenner's model in this way offers more evidence that anything and everything has the potential to influence brain development, whether positively or negatively, intentionally or unintentionally. If we draw all this together, we see yet more threads in relation to the critical role of the adult in relation to the developing brains of children:

The physical and emotional environments:
Contain multiple systems and contexts, etc.
These are influenced by the adults who inhabit (and, indeed, develop and create) children's worlds.
This is experienced by the child:
This influences the reactions of the various systems within the body.
And – is the difference between feeling stressed or safe.
In other words:
Adults impact on children's stress levels:
Positively or negatively.
Directly or indirectly, intentionally or unintentionally.

Which in turn:

Has a direct bearing on the developing brain.

Which brings us back to stress... We discussed stress in Chapter 1 and looked at what causes stress (stressors) and how levels of stress link to responses, such as fight, flight, or freeze, etc. Furthermore, neuroscience research has now evidenced how the human brain (and body) is physically altered by stress. The Center on the Developing Child at Harvard University offers the following overview (see also Chapter 6 and the web resources at the end of Chapter 1 for more):

> When external threats trigger the body's stress response, multiple systems spring into action like a team of highly skilled athletes, each with a specialized capability that complements the others. Systems relating to brain activity, heart and lung function, digestion, energy production, and fighting infection are all interconnected and influence each other's development.
>
> (Center on the Developing Child, 2022)

In other words, too much early brain stress can have far-reaching consequences. This evidence is growing – and brings into sharp focus how we, as adults, need to carefully consider and reflect on our roles in supporting brain development and minimising stress. Julie Denton is a childminder who works with a team of three practitioners. In this case study Julie discusses the importance of adults reflecting on potentially stressful situations for children:

Settling In? *It's a Walk in the Park*

Our transition/settling in process was a thoughtful one.... Or so we thought! We encouraged a couple of weeks of visits to the setting to stay and play, with the child's parent gradually withdrawing. However, a few years ago, we had the unusual situation where five young children all started at the setting within a three-month period.

Three of the children quickly demonstrated feelings of security and confidence within the setting, two found it more difficult, and needed time and intensive support before they were able to achieve a good level of well-being.

The children who struggled were a real concern for us. We know that in these circumstances the child is feeling real discomfort and distress, and experiencing stress. The practitioners felt this stress too, we needed to find ways to contain their emotions and support them to find comfort and security in their relationships with us. It is hard, intensive emotional work. I can remember as a child feeling acutely fearful in similar situations and do not want children who come to my setting to feel like this.

We reflected on the situation and considered how we might work to avoid this in the future.

To review the settling in process, we reflected as a team, and asked the parents of the five children for feedback. The answers were interesting. Parents described the positives and negatives of their experience settling their children. I noticed a clear difference between the families who 'settled well' and those who struggled. Notably the parents of the children who found transition most difficult said that their visits to the setting were hard for them, they felt uncomfortable and "like the first day at a new job". One dad said it was like being in an "alien environment".

Reflecting upon these conversations we considered the child, brought to an unfamiliar environment with new sounds, smells and noises, strange adults, and other children. We considered how children would be looking to their parent/carer to read their emotions, which will then shape the child's emotional reactions to us. In a nutshell if their parents are anxious and unsettled it is likely the child will feel the same.

Following this review process, we have changed our approach to transition/settling in. The pandemic of Covid-19 also helped us to significantly reconsider too. During periods of lock-down, we were unable to have visitors to the setting, instead meeting families wherever the parent was comfortable. We met in the park, or on a local walk and this worked really well.

We discuss our transition programme in the very first meeting when the parent is finding out about a potential place for their child. We believe this is crucial as it is a long process which could potentially affect the families' plans too. For example, we suggest avoiding settling in when other major changes are happening in the child's life.

Where possible we start to plan the transition two months before the child's start date. We contact the family and discuss our range of ideas for meeting and building relationships. We support the family to choose the ways they are most comfortable to spend time together. We explain clearly that the aims of settling-in meetings are to build relationships between the practitioner, the parent and the child. Here are the options and ideas we offer:

- We often start with a walk in the park, introduce us all to each other again and give a relaxed opportunity for chat and play. This may be repeated several times.
- We suggest a home visit. This gives the child the opportunity to see us in their safe place. This also reassures children that their parents have welcomed us, so we must be ok.
- We may introduce the child to the group of children by meeting on one of our outings, they can join in and play with us. This gives the parent the opportunity to see us working with the other children, which will also reassure them.
- We may take them out from the setting on a short local trip. This gives the child the experience of being transported differently but with the parent along too.
- We open the setting to parents visiting with the child, playing and spending time. These visits lengthen, incorporate lunch and maybe a sleep, so the child gets used to our routines before they start with us.
- Gradually the parent will withdraw, perhaps sitting in the kitchen filling in forms, etc. then leaving for extending periods.
- We tend to plan about 10/15 sessions of various types and then alter this to suit the child and family.

We have followed this plan now for several families and are really pleased with the results. The feedback from the parents is fabulous. From our point of view, I would say that whilst it is quite a big commitment the rewards are definitely worth it. This way builds a deeper and more authentic relationship with both the child and the family, even before their official start date. The children ease into attendance as if it is just another visit. Recently, one mum said to me that although she was dreading returning to work, she now feels excited for her son to come here more, and free to go back to work without any anxiety.

As adults, we have the potential to build or damage, to encourage or disapprove, to empower or impede... every single minute of every single day that we are interacting with children. In fact, it is wider than that, as Bronfenbrenner's model shows. When we support families, friends, neighbours, communities and when we work with other professionals and services, we can support the children that *they* come into contact with. And, when we listen to politicians, consider manifestoes, and decide where to put our votes, we have the potential to support the development of all children, and the contexts they grow up in.

> Two overarching concerns of infant mental health are the twin themes of development and context... these themes underscore how infants become who they are ... by developing within multiple contexts.
>
> (Zeanah, 2019: 1)

Adverse Influences on Brain Development

As we have considered, environments and relationships are crucial to brain development – and influence how both children and adults feel, behave and respond. There are of course, sadly, some difficulties. Science is now showing how the influences of illness, abuse, famine, poverty, deprivation, war, and discrimination, etc., can have unfavourable, adverse and harmful impacts on brain architecture.

REFLECTIVE PRACTICE

Disadvantage or Discrimination?

Let's consider a range of influences which can potentially impact brain development.

Let's imagine we have two families:

Family Circumstances		
Detail	*Family 1*	*Family 2*
Family	3 children – 6-month-old, 2-year-old and 4½-year-old 2 parents	2 children – 18-month-old and a 4½-year-old 2 parents
Home	Rented house in inner city Small garden	Large house in suburbs of city Large garden
Work	One parent works part-time in local supermarket Other parent is often out of work	One parent is a part-time teacher Other parent is an accountant
Childcare	Children access childcare/ school Grandma helps out when she can	Children access childcare/ school Parents pay for additional hours Children spend one day a week with grandparents

Now let's consider some influences that could potentially cause difficulties for families.

Potential Influences		
Parent Focussed	*Child Focussed*	*Wider Influences*
One parent is made redundant	The family have adopted the children	A grandparent dies

One parent becomes seriously ill and has to spend time in hospital	One of the children is diagnosed with a life-threatening illness	There is increasing violence in the local neighbourhood
One of the parents has a disability	The children are 'fussy eaters'	Access to local healthcare is difficult
One parent is imprisoned	There is suspicions of abuse or domestic abuse	The country finds itself at war
Mum is having another baby	The childcare/school closes	The heating stops working, and there is no hot water
The parents decide to permanently separate	One of the children has a disability	The country experiences a severe shortage of food staples such as bread, pasta, and rice
One parent gets a job on the other side of town	The local park closes	There is an issue with prostitution, drugs, and alcohol locally
There is a history of post-natal depression	The children often miss days of childcare/school	The family move house, to a new community

Pick any one of the potential influences, from any of the boxes and consider how it could impact on family 1 and family 2.

1. What support might the family have?
   a. Financial support?
   b. Emotional support?
   c. Practical day-to-day support?
      i. How could this impact on the parents?
      ii. How could this impact on the children?
2. What could the potential impact(s) be?
   a. How might this add stress to the family?
      i. For the parents?
      ii. For the children?

3. Do you notice any differences in the potential impacts on the two families?
   a. Why do you think that is?
4. Any other thoughts?

And finally:

5. How might all of this impact on the brain development of the children within each family?

If we consider there can be two or three, or more, potential influences impacting on some families at any one time, it becomes easy to see how the pressure mounts. Living in poverty adds to the stress:

> [A] combination of pressures and the lack of financial lifelines such as credit, savings or help from family that sweeps us into poverty and leaves us fighting every day.
>
> (Joseph Rowntree Foundation, 2022: 4)

Now consider, what if the following also applied to one of the families:

The parents struggle with reading English
The parents are teenagers
Dad is the main child-carer
The parents are same sex
The family speaks English as an additional language
One parent undergoes gender reassignment
The family is black, Jewish, Chinese, mixed-heritage, Mormon, Muslim, Traveller heritage, Arabic or from other cultural or religious backgrounds
The family are asylum seekers

If you were to reconsider the 1-5 questions in the reflective practice exercise in relation to the bullet point list, the answers could be very, very different! In the U.K. (which is the fifth largest economy in the world) there should not be a correlation between the potential stressors in the grid in the reflective practice exercise and the bullet point list. The data clearly shows that there is:

> Despite such increases in family diversity and complexity, society – as well as the systems within society, such as the legal, health care, and school systems – have continued to prize the heteronormative nuclear biological family ideal [one mum and one dad], thus potentially marginalizing LG [lesbian/gay] parent families and adoptive parent families.
>
> (Goldberg, 2014: 669)

> Although all families are vulnerable to poverty some are more affected than others; … 47 per cent of lone-parent families live in poverty.
>
> (CPAG, 2018; Marsh et al., 2017)

> Family poverty is highly gendered – 90 per cent of lone-parents are women and are at higher risk due to limited work opportunities.
>
> (Alston, 2018; Millar and Ridge, 2013)

> Black, Asian and Minority Ethnic (BAME) groups are twice as likely as white groups to live in poverty due to intersecting issues of unemployment, economic

activity, lower pay, geographic location, migration status and educational attainment. (Joseph Rowntree Foundation, 2017)

Lyndon, 2019: 603)

Children birth through age five are exposed to disproportionate rates of certain types of adversity compared to older children, including maltreatment (U.S. Department of Health and Human Services, Administration for Children and Families, Administration on Children Youth and Families, Children's Bureau, 2018) and domestic violence (Fantuzzo and Fusco, 2007). Higher rates of cumulative adversities have also been found for young ethnic minority children and children living in poverty (Jimenez et al., 2016; Mersky et al., 2013).

(Loomis, 2021: 229)

The poverty rate for individuals who live in families where someone is disabled is 31%, 12 percentage points higher than those who live in families where no-one is disabled. Of all families in poverty, just under half contain someone who is disabled.

(Joseph Rowntree Foundation, 2022: 58)

I would urge you to explore the names and data in these quotes, and also in the bibliography to further develop your own knowledge. There is only so much room in this book and I acknowledge that we are only lightly touching on these very deep issues. However, it is important that we highlight some of these topics. Even from this short section it should be obvious, from the amount of data/figures, names, and references, etc. in the quotes, the depth of research that is available. The data, statistics and information clearly indicate the disproportionate impacts of poverty on some groups. If we add in families who are further disadvantaged because of discrimination (hence the title of the reflective practice exercise), the stressors multiply. The impact of discrimination increases the impacts of disadvantage. In other words, any one of the potential influences in the grid in the reflective practice exercise could be a pressure point (stressor) for either family. However, when we add in the points in the bullet list, this then potentially makes it harder to access support, which makes the stressors worse – for *both* families. In other words, potential stressors are made worse by the impacts of discrimination.

The Impacts of Discrimination

As we saw in the earlier quotes, for families who face discrimination in relation to their age, marital status, language, ethnicity, religion, gender, skin colour, sexuality, abilities, health needs, and so on, the disadvantage worsens. Let's explore what this could mean for families.

To begin with, let's consider the four main forms of discrimination – direct, indirect, victimisation and harassment.

> Direct discrimination – treating someone with a protected characteristic [see following bullet list] less favourably than others
>
> Indirect discrimination – putting rules or arrangements in place that apply to everyone, but that put someone with a protected characteristic at an unfair disadvantage
>
> Harassment – unwanted behaviour linked to a protected characteristic that violates someone's dignity or creates an offensive environment for them
>
> Victimisation – treating someone unfairly because they've complained about discrimination or harassment.
>
> (U.K. Government, 2022)

In addition, the protected characteristics are defined by the Equality Act (2010), and cover:

> Age
> Disability
> Gender reassignment (transgender)
> Marriage and civil partnership
> Pregnancy and maternity
> Race (colour, nationality, ethnic or national origin, etc.)
> Religion or belief
> Sex (gender)
> Sexual orientation (LGBTQIA+)

There is clear evidence linking discrimination and stressors on the role of adults in children's lives:

Multiple studies have documented how the stresses of everyday discrimination on parents or other caregivers, such as being associated with negative stereotypes, can have harmful effects on caregiving behaviors and adult mental health. And when caregivers' mental health is affected, the challenges of coping with it can cause an excessive stress response in their children.

(Center on the Developing Child, 2022)

Let's consider what this might mean in terms of early childhood practice.

REFLECTIVE PRACTICE
Anti-Discriminatory Practice

Anti-discriminatory practice is about more than equal opportunities, it is actively taking action to challenge discrimination. Gaias et al. (2021: 274) discuss the aims of anti-discriminatory practice to:

challenge the power relationships that create and sustain inequities in education. … change practice and policy in order to challenge existing power structures [and] empower all children to champion diversity and challenge discrimination. … classroom images and materials promote positive messages regarding diversity and inclusion.

They go on to highlight the importance of supporting and empowering children to know and recognise:

their own and others' identities, … classroom environments meaningfully reflect … backgrounds and perspectives… explicitly and proactively counteract discrimination and oppression … communicated both verbally and visually. Activities, interactions, and policies allow children to participate in decision-making based on their understanding of the world and their place within it.

(Gaias et al., 2021: 275)

Consider the following questions in terms of anti-discriminatory practice:

How do we actively advocate anti-discriminatory practices and challenge discrimination in terms of the following protected characteristics?
Age
Disability
Gender reassignment (transgender)
Marriage and civil partnership
Pregnancy and maternity
Race (colour, nationality, ethnic or national origin, etc.)
Religion or belief
Sex (gender)
Sexual orientation (LGBTQIA+)
Is anti-discriminatory practice visible in everyday practice in terms of:
Activities?
The environments (indoors/outdoors and physical/emotional)?
Images and materials?
Language and interactions?
Policies?
Staffing structures (covering all areas)?
What works well?
What needs further development?
Do *all* children, families and staff feel included and valued?
How do you know?
Anything else?

We can all have positive (or negative) influences on children, the setting, the families we work with, our colleagues, and the communities where we live and work. Things such as the language we use, our actions, and the environments we provide all send messages – what those messages are, is up to us.

By carefully considering our practices, we have the opportunity to be the supportive buffers needed where potentially stressful influences could become toxic stressors. We can see this clearly in our practice with children:

> The toddler who has learned that the people she depends on for comfort will help her when she is distressed is more likely to approach others with empathy and trust than the toddler whose worries and fears have been dismissed or belittled.
>
> (Shonkoff and Phillips, 2000: 90)

However, this 'ripple effect' is also much, much wider. When we support children, we have the potential to influence families, and colleagues within the setting, our communities and beyond. For example, we can offer support for people to access the help they need, through signposting to other agencies. Or, when we challenge inappropriate language in one place, that potentially has the power to change language used elsewhere. When we support someone to share their opinions and thoughts, they are more likely to do this elsewhere. When we provide environments where everyone feels included and valued, this demonstrates the importance of the environment to others, and is more likely to be replicated elsewhere.

We all have choices to make every day. As we have seen from the discussions here and elsewhere, stress has a direct correlation with brain development. Deprivation, adversity, discrimination, and poverty make the impact of stress worse. Therefore, brain development and child development are directly influenced by the choices we, as adults, make. If we go back to the quote we discussed earlier:

> The easiest and most effective way to support a child's development is by providing the best possible learning [development] environments as consistently as possible in all aspects of their life – in the home and family, at nursery [or setting], at school, and in our wider culture and society.
>
> (Goswami, 2020: xix)

Any one of the potential influences in the reflective practice grid could have happened to any one of us – or they *could* happen to any one of us at any time. The grid is almost a lottery, we never know what life is going to throw at us – and what the implications could be. The key message here is – it does not have to become toxic stress. The difference between stressful situations tipping from tolerable into toxic is having someone to buffer those impacts. Someone who uses serve and return interactions, someone who co-regulates to help us with our feelings, emotions, behaviours, and actions, etc. in order that we can self-regulate and use our executive functions. When this happens regularly and consistently, we build resilience – which helps us to cope with what life is throwing at us. This is true for children, for adults, for families, for communities – for all humans, and it starts in early childhood:

> Professors Chris Pascal and Tony Bertram (2016), from the Centre for Research in Early Childhood (CREC), released the findings from their High Achieving, White Working Class Boys (HAWWC Boys) project.
>
> … project identified a group of approximately 40 boys, who, at the end of the reception year of school, were achieving academically, despite some very difficult, traumatic, and chaotic home lives. But and this is hugely important, not only were this group of boys achieving well, they were achieving in the top percentage in the country, and outstripping some of their more affluent peers. …
>
> Supporting and sustaining strong, secure and trusting attachments of young boys to key adults and peers, both within and outside of their home, is critical to healthy development, resilience and wellbeing.
>
> Building in regular and sustained periods of outdoor and physical activity will enhance the young boy's learning, motivation and wellbeing (Pascal and Bertram, 2016: 16).
>
> (Garvey, 2018: 184)

The HAWWC study is incredibly important, and I would urge you to explore the wealth of materials on the website (see bibliography). One of the key findings, as mentioned in the quote, was the importance of outdoor play. As we've discussed elsewhere, play matters (both indoors and outdoors), and is vital to early brain development. Which, in terms of this chapter, brings us nicely to the role of adults and play.

Adults and Play

As you may have noticed elsewhere, I am fascinated by what we, as humans, can learn from the animal world. This is particularly true when it comes to play and adults. Play in the animal world is vital for developing skills needed as adults. Play is mainly about species survival, and in the majority of species is limited to the young:

> Playful behaviour gradually drops out ... of the monkey as it matures. Most adult male monkeys rarely, if ever, play, and the situation is similar for adult females although they may interact playfully with their infants. ... Why does it drop out along the way and why don't adults play?
>
> (Dolinhow, 1971: 512)

I read that final sentence with a rueful smile... and think how easily (and sadly) that could be transferred to many adults in the human world. In terms of play, the role of the adult is vital, whether for young monkeys or children:

> [Children] are designed to learn about the real world that surrounds them, and they learn by playing with the things in that world, most of all by playing with the people who love them.
>
> (Gopnik et al., 2001: 201)

Meanwhile, Professor Jerome Bruner (1915–2016) lamented the lack of some adults' understanding regarding the importance of play:

> Technological societies ... as they become increasingly developed. ... made very early a sharp separation between what one does when young and what one does later, with the transition very sharply defined.
>
> In the western tradition there grew a puritan separation of the "works of the adult" and "the play of babes". But it was clear to both sides what the two were about.
>
> Now "the play of the babes" has become separate from, dissociated from, the adult community and not understood by that community any better than the young comprehend or accept the ideals of the adult community.
>
> (Bruner, 1971: 82)

We have also explored how play matters in terms of brain development (in fact, it matters so much there is a whole chapter on it). Therefore, if we have agreed that play matters to brain development, and in this chapter, we have discussed how the role of the adult is vital to brain development, then I think we can safely say that they are both equally vital.

REFLECTIVE PRACTICE
Adults and Play

Find a nice quiet place to think about this one. Then, think of a play memory from your childhood. If you can, close your eyes and really explore your memories…

Think of a play memory – a time in your childhood where you were having fun with an adult(s). Try and really explore it in your mind.

Now consider the following:

Where are you?
Are you indoors or outdoors?
What can you see, smell, hear and so on?
What are the adult(s) doing/not doing?
What are the adult(s) saying/not saying?
How did you feel?

Now consider the following:

Imagine, in 10, 20 or even 50 years' time – someone somewhere asks people to do this same activity – and the person they remember is you!

I do this activity when I am delivering training all the time. Initially, when I ask people to close their eyes, they look a little worried. I reassure the group that it is not scary, and I am not going to shout 'boo'. Once I start talking and ask people to consider a play memory, the room feels as if it is being held in a warm, comforting, loving hug.

As I talk through the questions, people begin to smile (still with their eyes closed). As I continue with the questions, I can see the feelings and emotions on people's faces. When I finish talking and ask people to open their eyes, and if anyone is willing to share their reflections, some people are visibly moved to tears. Not because they are sad, but because they have had the opportunity to revisit a joyous memory with a much-loved adult.

Sometimes, the people we remember in our play memories are grandparents, or perhaps people who are no longer with us. Sometimes the people are parents, aunts or uncles or other family members. Sometimes the memories are of childminders, nursery staff, teachers, and other professionals. Whoever the adults are – they played a critical part in our childhoods… and a critical part in our brain development.

On training, I usually ask people to then work in small groups to consider what they think they might have been learning during the play experiences they had considered. For your own reflections you might want to consider this too. Have a think about the areas of learning and development; you might be surprised at how many you were covering in your own play memory. (And, as an aside – did it feel like learning to that child in your memory?)

Here we are back again at the critical nature of empowering, encouraging and supportive environments where we know we are loved, being supported by interested adults. In terms of neuroscience, the evidence now shows that these elements enable us to develop our knowledge, skills, experiences, and understanding, in a way that makes sense to us, and to our brains. In other words, it is how we *feel* that is the key.

There is a saying that I use a lot, the origins of which are a little lost in the fog of time. So, either, Maya Angelou, Carl W. Buehner or Carol Bucher, said:

I've learnt that:

People will forget what you said,
People will forget what you did, but…
People will never forget how you made them feel.

… and the same goes for children… To use my favourite Bronfenbrenner quote again, but this time, bear in mind – this could be you!

> In order to develop normally, a child requires progressively more complex joint activity with one or more adults… *Every child needs at least one adult who is irrationally crazy about him or her.*

Chapter Reflection

Thinking back over this chapter, consider the various elements (sections, quotes, reflective exercises, terminology, etc.). Are there any elements that:

Were particularly useful?
Need re-reading, or more thought or reflection?
You want to look up and/or explore further?

Any other thoughts or reflections?

Bibliography

The following are books, articles, web pages, organisations, documents, etc. that I have found useful (online versions, all accessed 20 July 2022). Some are directly referenced in this chapter – some are included as valuable sources of background reading that might be helpful. See also web resources at the end of Chapter 1.

Ackerman, C. E. (2018) What is self-regulation? (+95 skills and strategies). *Positive Psychology.* [blog] 3 July. Available at: https://positivepsychology.com/self-regulation/.

Alston, P. (2018) *Statement on Visit to the United Kingdom, by Professor Philip Alston, United Nations Special Rapporteur on Extreme Poverty and Human Rights.* 16 November 2018. London. Available at: https://www.ohchr.org/EN/NewsEvents/Pages/DisplayNews.aspx?NewsID=23881&LangID=E.

Bronfenbrenner, U. (1977) Toward an experimental ecology of human development. *American Psychologist*, 32, pp. 513–531. Available at: https://psycnet.apa.org/doi/10.1037/0003-066X.32.7.513.

Bronfenbrenner, U. (1979) *The Ecology of Human Development*. Cambridge, MA: Harvard University Press.

Bronfenbrenner, U. (1992) *Ecological Systems Theory*. London: Jessica Kingsley Publishers.

Bronfenbrenner, U. (1999) Environments in developmental perspective: theoretical and operational models. In: S. L. Friedman and T. D. Wachs, eds. *Measuring Environment Across the Lifespan: Emerging Methods and Concepts*. Washington, DC: American Psychological Association Press, pp. 3–28.

Bronfenbrenner, U. and Ceci, S. J. (1994) Nature-nurture reconceptualized in developmental perspective: a bioecological model. *Psychological Review*, 101, pp. 568–586. Available at: https://doi.org/10.1037/0033-295x.101.4.568.

Child Poverty Action Group [CPAG]. (2018) *Who Lives in Poverty? Child Poverty Facts and Figures*. London: CPAG. Available at http://www.cpag.org.uk/content/who-lives-poverty.

Early Education. (2021) *Birth to 5 Matters: Non-statutory Guidance for the Early Years Foundation Stage*. St. Albans: Early Education (On behalf of Early years Coalition).

Equality Act 2010. Available at: https://www.legislation.gov.uk/ukpga /2010/15/contents.

Fantuzzo, J. W. and Fusco, R. A. (2007) Children's direct exposure to types of domestic violence crime: a population based investigation. *Journal of Family Violence*, 22(7), pp. 543–552. Available at: https://doi.org/10.1007/s10896-007-9105-z.

Gaias, L. M., Gal-Szabo, D. E., Shivers, E. M. and Kiche, S. (2021) From laissez-faire to anti-discrimination: how are race/ethnicity, culture, and bias integrated into multiple domains of practice in early childhood education? *Journal of Research in Childhood Education*, 36(2), pp. 272–295. Available at: https://doi.org/10.1080/02568543 .2021.1951403.

Garvey, D. (2018) *Nurturing Personal, Social and Emotional Development in Early Childhood: A Practical Guide to Understanding Brain Development and Young Children's Behaviour*. London: Jessica Kingsley Publishers.

Goldberg, A. E. (2014) Lesbian, gay, and heterosexual adoptive parents' experiences in preschool environments. *Early Childhood Research Quarterly*, 29(4), pp. 669–681. Available at: https://doi.org/10.1016/j.ecresq.2014.07.008.

Gopnik, A., Meltzoff, A. N. and Kuhl, P. K. (2001) *How Babies Think: The Science of Childhood*. London: Phoenix.

Goswami, U. (2020) *Cognitive Development and Cognitive Neuroscience: The Learning Brain*. 2nd edn. Abingdon: Routledge.

Henry-Allain, L. and Lloyd-Rose, M. (2022) The Tiney guide to becoming an inclusive, anti-racist early educator. [e-book]. Tiney. Available at: https://assets.ctfassets.net/jnn9p19md0ig/4ntGEh2 1KNXyB9aLxq9gCY/61847fa97f563ba4d9b281cf89d8a8ef/Guide_Inclusive_Education.pdf.

Jimenez, M. E., Wade, R., Lin, Y., Morrow, L. M. and Reichman, N. E. (2016) Adverse experiences in early childhood and kindergarten outcomes. *Pediatrics*, 137(2), pp. 1–11. Available at: https://doi.org/10.1542/peds.2015-1839.

Joseph Rowntree Foundation. (2017) *Poverty and Ethnicity in the Labour Market*. [pdf]. York: Joseph Rowntree Foundation. Available at https://www.jrf.org.uk/report/poverty-ethnicity-labour-market.

Joseph Rowntree Foundation (2022) *U.K. Poverty Report 2022: The Essential Guide to Understanding Poverty in the U.K.* [pdf]. York: Joseph Rowntree Foundation. Available at: https://www.jrf.org.uk/report/uk-poverty-2022.

Loomis, A. M. (2021) Effects of household and environmental adversity on indices of self-regulation for Latino and African American preschool children: closing the school readiness gap. *Early Education and Development*, 32(2), pp. 228–248. Available at: https://doi.org/10.1080/10409289.2020.1745513.

Lyndon, S. (2019) Troubling discourses of poverty in early childhood in the U.K. *Children and Society*, 33(6), pp. 602–609. Available at: https://doi.org/10.1111/chso.12354.

Marsh, A., Barker, K., Ayrton, C., Treanor, M. and Haddad, M. (2017) *Poverty: The Facts.* 6th edn. London: Child Poverty Action Group.

Mersky, J. P., Topitzes, J. and Reynolds, A. J. (2013) Impacts of adverse childhood experiences on health, mental health, and substance use in early adulthood: a cohort study of an urban, minority sample in the U.S. *Child Abuse and Neglect*, 37(11), pp. 917–925. Available at: https://doi.org/10.1016/j.chiabu.2013.07.011.

Millar, J. and Ridge, T. (2013) Lone mothers and paid work: the family-work project. *International Review of Sociology*, 23(3), pp. 564–577. Available at: https://doi.org/10.1080/03906701.2013.856161.

Millar, K. (2019) What is delayed gratification and how do you pass the Marshmallow test? *Positive Psychology.* [blog] 30 December. Available at: https://positivepsychology.com/delayed-gratification/.

Minh, A., Muhajarine, N., Janus, M., Brownell, M. and Guhn, M. (2017) A review of neighborhood effects and early child development: how, where, and for whom, do neighborhoods matter? *Health and Place*, 46, pp. 155–174. Available at: https://doi.org/10.1016/j.healthplace.2017.04.012.

Pascal, C. and Bertram, T. (2016) *High Achieving White Working Class (HAWWC) Boys Project: Final Report.* Birmingham: CREC (Centre for Research in Early Childhood). Available at: https://www.crec.co.uk/hawwc-boys.

Page, J. (2011) Do mothers want professional carers to love their babies? *Journal of Early Childhood Research*, 9(3), pp. 310–323.

Page, J. (2014) Developing professional love in early childhood settings. In: L. Harrison and J. Sumsion, eds. *International Perspectives on Early Childhood and Development: Lived Spaces of Infant-Toddler Education and Care: Exploring Diverse Perspectives on Theory, Research and Practice.* Dordrecht, NL: Springer, pp. 119–130.

Page, J. (2016) Educators' perspectives on attachment and professional love in early years settings in England. In: E. J. White and C. Dalli, eds. *Under Three-Year-Olds in Policy and Practice. Policy and Pedagogy with Under-Three-Year-Olds: Cross-Disciplinary Insights and Innovations for Educational Research with Very Young Children Series*. Dordrecht, NL: Springer, pp. 131–142.

Page, J. (2017) Reframing infant-toddler pedagogy through a lens of professional love: exploring narratives of professional practice in early childhood settings in England. *Contemporary Issues in Early Childhood*, 18(4), pp. 387–399.

Shonkoff, J. P. and Phillips, D. A., eds. (2000) *From Neurons to Neighborhoods: The Science of Early Childhood Development*. Washington, DC: National Academy Press.

Shonkoff, J. P., Slopen, N. and Williams, D. R. (2021) Early childhood adversity, toxic stress, and the impacts of racism on the foundations of health. *Annual Review of Public Health*, 42, pp. 115–134. Available at: https://doi.org/10.1146/annurev-publhealth-090419-101940.

U.K. Government (2022) *Discrimination: Your Rights*. Available at: https://www.gov.uk/discrimination-your-rights/how-you-can-be-discriminated-against.

U.S. Department of Health and Human Services, Administration for Children and Families, Administration on Children Youth and Families, Children's Bureau (2018) *Child Maltreatment 2016* [archived]. Available at: https://www.acf.hhs.gov/cb/report/child-maltreatment-2016.

Wright, D. (2022) Benign neglect. *Siren Films*. [blog]. Available at: https://www.sirenfilms.co.uk/benign-neglect/.

Zeanah, C. H. (2019) *Handbook of Infant Mental Health*. 4th edn. New York: The Guilford Press.

The following can be found in:

Bruner, J. S., Jolly, A. and Sylva, K., eds. (2017) *Play Its Role in Development and Evolution*. New York: Basic Books. (Available as: e-Book 2017 International Psychotherapy Institute). Available at: https://www.researchgate.net/publication/328486788_Play_its_role_in_development_and_evolution.

Dolinhow, P. (1971) At play in the fields. (From a Special Supplement of the Natural History Magazine, December 1971). In: J. S. Bruner, A. Jolly and K. Sylva, eds. *Play Its Role in Development and Evolution*. New York: Basic Books. (Available as: e-Book 2017 International Psychotherapy Institute).

In early childhood and across education, there are several terms we use when exploring social and emotional development:

PSED – Personal, Social and Emotional Development
PSHE – Personal, Social and Health Education
IMH – Infant Mental Health
SEMH – Social, Emotional and Mental Health

And probably a whole host of others – for this chapter, and in line with other books in the Little Minds Matter series, we are going to use the term SEMH – Social, Emotional and Mental Health.

REFLECTIVE PRACTICE

Defining 'Social, Emotional and Mental Health'?

Think about the term 'Social, Emotional and Mental Health'.

Here are some questions to help your reflections:

What do you think of when you consider the term 'Social, Emotional and Mental Health'?

DOI: 10.4324/9781003154846-6

What words, thoughts, and feelings spring to mind?
Have you heard it used? (How, Where, Why, When?)
Any other thoughts or reflections?

There are no right/wrong answers – this is about your experiences and reflections.

In my experience, when faced with trying to define something, the dictionary is often the best place to start. It can be helpful to break down a phrase into specific words:

Social
  In relation to a specific situation/society/culture
  Interactions, friendships, and relationships
  Taking turns, sharing, give-and-take
Emotional
  In relation to feelings, emotions, and behaviours
  Recognise, understand, and express emotions appropriately
  Knowing what is acceptable in a specific situation/culture
Mental
  In relation to the mind, intellect, and the brain
  Thinking
  An offensive term for illness or impairment
Health
  In relation to levels of mental or physical welfare
  State of wellbeing
  Originates from the word hale (hence the term 'hale and hearty')

These seemingly wide-ranging definitions actually give us some interesting starting points, and there are certainly some words that sound familiar to our early childhood world. In terms of the definition of 'mental', I am sure none of us would intentionally use the term offensively. However, I do wonder how many of us use it as a 'throwaway comment', without considering how it could be perceived. Phrases such as 'it's mental in here', or 'I'm going mental worrying about my assignment' are heard in everyday language. Using language such as this lacks compassion, does not help to break down the stigma, and can be seen as trivialising.

In terms of a more specific definition of the phrase 'mental health', there are a whole host of organisations that you can explore at your leisure. Firstly though, it might be useful to consider the global definition of 'mental health' as defined by the World Health Organization (WHO):

> Mental health is an integral and essential component of health. The WHO constitution states: "Health is a state of complete physical, mental and social well-being and not merely the absence of disease or infirmity." An important implication of this definition is that mental health is more than just the absence of mental disorders or disabilities.
>
> Mental health is a state of well-being in which an individual realizes his or her own abilities, can cope with the normal stresses of life, can work productively and is able to make a contribution to his or her community.
>
> (WHO, 2018 [no page])

This offers some useful pointers in terms of our understanding in early childhood. Again, there are words and phrases that feel very familiar. If we move on to look specifically at the word 'health', Sartorius (2006: 662) offers a useful overview of the range of definitions available:

> absence of ... disease or impairment. ....
> a state that allows the individual to adequately cope with all demands of daily life (implying also the absence of disease and impairment). ...
> a state of balance ... that an individual has established within himself and between himself and his social and physical environment.

The phrase SEMH is usually associated with school-aged children, and particularly with children with special educational needs and disabilities (SEND). However, there is growing recognition of the need to consider this area further within early childhood.

Sonia Mainstone-Cotton has written extensively on this subject, and I do not intend to simply repeat it here. I would urge you to explore Sonia's work, and we can start by considering the following, regarding SEMH in childhood:

> Children who find it difficult to manage their feelings, emotions and behaviours
> Children who find everyday change challenging and frightening
> Children who find it difficult to build relationships with adults or children
> Children who find it hard to join in the activities and routine with the rest of the class/group.
>
> (Mainstone-Cotton, 2021: 7)

Bearing all of this in mind, we can safely presume that social, emotional and mental health has a place in early childhood discussions. We are interested in wellbeing, physical/emotional/social abilities, how we cope with normal stresses of life, impact of our environments, our communities – and the impacts of SEND, or diseases/impairments/injuries, etc. I am also sure we have all met children (and indeed adults) who find some of this difficult. Of course, supporting SEMH in early childhood links strongly with environments, play, the role of the adult and other chapters in this book. In some ways, this chapter is an amalgamation of topics touched on elsewhere. I suppose that kind of makes sense; after all, our SEMH relies on everything else around us. Wherever possible I have made links to other chapters – and in other chapters made links to here. My sincere apologies if I have missed any. However, for the purposes of this chapter, we are going to concentrate on the impact of change and the importance of consistency – for children and adults:

> We are all on an SEMH needs continuum and we all need to have our SEMH needs met.
>
> (Mainstone-Cotton, 2021: 1)

Learning from Neuroscience: Impacts on SEMH

In simplistic terms, the reptilian brain controls our bodily functions and our responses to what is happening around us (especially danger). The reptilian brain needs food, warmth, sleep, routine and people who help it to feel safe, and once all these things are in place the reptilian section of the brain feels secure.

(Garvey, 2018: 37)

Let's explore this a bit further, and start by considering the basic human needs of warmth, sleep and shelter:

REFLECTIVE PRACTICE

Reptilian Reactions and Relationships and Routines (Part 1)

Let's consider some of the key elements in more depth:
Food/Warmth/Sleep/Shelter
Think about how you behave/react when you are too hungry/ too hot/too cold/too tired, away from home, etc.
What helps?
What makes things harder?

Yes, I know some of the answers to these questions are 'depends on what/ why it happened/where I am/who I am with' type scenarios. However, on the whole, we are not usually at our best when we are tired, hungry, and/ or cold, etc.

REFLECTIVE PRACTICE

Reptilian Reactions and Relationships and Routines (Part 2)

Now consider:
Routines/Relationships
How do your routines/relationships around you help (or not, as the case may be)?
How do you feel, how do you react?
Do you react/behave differently depending on where you are, or who you are with?
Why do you think that is?

I suspect that many of us will be able to identify when routines and relationships helped when we were finding things difficult (or didn't help, as the case may be). The colleague who brings a cool drink when it is too hot, the partner who offers to cook, or the manager who supervises lunchtime so we can have a breather. The fact that we *know* it is only a short time until lunchtime, or bedtime, or that it's nearly the weekend. All of these relationships and routines tell the reptilian brain that we are safe – because things are consistent. If that seems like a big leap, then imagine the opposite. The people who do not seem to notice we need support (or do not care). Or if we do not know when the next meal is, or when/where we will be able to sleep safely for example. It feels uncomfortable writing this – we are teetering on the edges of poverty and abuse here... But... that is exactly why the reptilian brain needs to feel secure. We are born programmed to survive. After all, if we do not have enough food/warmth, etc., it would be perfectly understandable for the reptilian brain to be worried about our very survival.

Many ... environmental factors [which support] brain functioning are everyday matters – the quality of social environment ... interactions, nutrition, physical exercise ... sleep – ... seem too obvious and easily overlooked ... holistic approaches which recognise the close interdependence of physical and intellectual well-being and ... of the emotional and cognitive.

(OECD, 2002: 76)

As humans are born so vulnerable, we are reliant on people around us who care. Therefore, when these things are missing or inconsistent, this tips us into high-alert mode and the fight, flight, freeze, etc., we discussed in Chapter 1. This is a biological response design to protect us and keep us alive.

Science can now help us understand why – and the wider implications. Let's look at this firstly from a purely biological point of view. The National Institute for Health and Care Excellence (NICE) is a U.K. organisation providing information, evidence-based guidance and advice designed to improve outcomes for health and social care and offers a range of resources.

Food

Clearly, food is vital for humans. We eat a number of calories, which are turned into the energy which is fuel for our bodies to work. Eating the 'right' amount can be a challenge for many people, and the implications are far reaching. The biological science is clear:

Excess weight may increase the risk of coronary heart disease, hypertension [High Blood Pressure], liver disease, osteoarthritis, stroke, type 2 diabetes, and some cancers such as breast, colon, endometrial and kidney cancer. People who are overweight or obese may also experience mental health problems, stigmatisation and discrimination because of their weight.

(NICE Quality Standard [QS24], 13 March 2015)

When people are malnourished, their basic health and social care outcomes are significantly affected, making malnutrition an important patient safety issue. It continues to be both under-detected and undertreated, with potentially fatal consequences.

(NICE Guideline [NG7], 30 November 2015)

Warmth

I am sure we all have experiences of being too hot, or too cold, it can be uncomfortable either way. However, it can also be life threatening:

A wide range of people are vulnerable to the cold. This is either because of: a medical condition, such as heart disease; a disability that, for instance, stops people moving around to keep warm, or makes them more likely to develop chest infections; or personal circumstances, such as being unable to afford to keep warm enough.

In this guideline, the term vulnerable refers to a number of groups including:

people with cardiovascular conditions
people with respiratory conditions (in particular, chronic obstructive pulmonary disease and childhood asthma)
people with mental health conditions
people with disabilities
older people (65 and older)
households with young children (from new–born to school age)
pregnant women
people on a low income.

(NICE Guideline [NG6], 05 March 2015)

Likewise, being too hot is dangerous too. As I sit here writing this, the U.K. Met Office has issued a RED extreme heat warning for the first time, as temperatures are expected to reach 40°C in the next few days (Faulkner, 2022 [no page]). The warning is clear – temperatures as high as this pose a threat to life.

Sleep

I am sure we are all fully aware of how we feel after a sleepless night. The nights where we have lain awake worrying about something specific, or those nights where our minds race around and we seem unable to switch off. However, constant (chronic) insomnia has implications on our wider health:

Short-term insomnia is common and can occur in association with stressful events or changes in sleeping patterns such as illness, financial difficulties, the birth of a child or environmental disturbance.

Chronic insomnia commonly co-exists with other psychiatric and medical conditions (for example anxiety, depression, and COPD [Chronic Obstructive Pulmonary Disease]).

(NICE Health Topics: Insomnia, February 2022)

Clearly, we are not going to die from missing the odd meal, or a night or two of difficulty sleeping. This is about how not having safe, regular, consistent food/warmth/sleep/shelter, etc. has serious biological, physical health implications – and the impact this has on SEMH. It's the words 'safe, regular and consistent' that we are interested in for this chapter. As we mentioned earlier, ever alert to potential threats or dangers, the reptilian area of the brain (or brainstem) prefers consistency.

REFLECTIVE PRACTICE
Change vs Consistency

Rahul is very excited about his third birthday coming up at the end of May. Rahul is generally happy and chatty. Rahul is always excited when any new equipment arrives. Rahul is usually the first to speak to any new children, staff, or visitors.

Now consider:

Mid-May	Rahul's dad gets a new job and has to work longer hours, meaning a change of mealtimes.
August	The family has a new baby, and sometimes Rahul finds it difficult to sleep.
January	The heating breaks down and cannot be fixed for several weeks as a new part needs ordering.

Imagine if the timeline in the grid happens to Rahul:
How might this influence Rahul's SEMH?
What reactions/behaviours might you see?

Then consider if one or more of the following happens:

Rahul's family goes on holiday for 2 weeks.
Rahul's key person is going on extended leave for a month, for a minor operation/recovery.
Rahul's favourite teddy is missing.
Rahul's friend moves to another part of the country.

What might you need to consider in terms of:

The physical environment?
The emotional environment?
The adults involved (parents and practitioners)?

In the previous reflective practice exercise 'Reptilian Reactions and Relationships and Routines' we explored how it feels for us as adults – and how it can be difficult for us, even though we *usually* have the skills to be able to cope. For children, these situations can be much harder. In terms of Rahul, I am sure you will be able to clearly define some of the reactions (or behaviours) we might see over a period of time. The key here is to remember – this is a biological reaction. We need to bear in mind that for the reptilian brain:

Change can be challenging
Consistency is vital
Relationships are key

This does not mean that things can never change, or routines must be rigid. It is more that inconsistencies and unexpected change cause worries. 'A change is as good as a rest', as the saying goes – and that is also true. In fact, for the majority of people, too much rigidness isn't helpful either, brains need challenge, excitement, and stimulation in order to develop. This is about balance. And this is where relationships become vital – because it is relationships that help us to deal with change and inconsistencies and find our balance. As adults, we can usually do this as we have previous experiences and strategies that have helped us to learn how to deal with our emotions, and so be able to self-regulate. However, children need help – known as co-regulation (which we will come back to shortly) – and for this, relationships are key. We looked at the role of adults in depth in the previous chapter, and we'll come back to regulation and co-regulation shortly. For now, let's just consider the importance of relationships specifically in the context of neuroscience, SEMH and change and consistency.

The Importance of Relationships

The way humans form relationships is based on thousands (or maybe even millions) of micro-connections. Our brains are pre-programmed to respond to those micro-connections. For us as adults, as an example, it might be helpful to think about when you meet someone new for the first time. We generally use eye contact, facial expressions and so on, to make connections, and to see if the other person is someone we could, or want to, form a relationship with. Our body language may (unconsciously) start to mirror what the other person is doing. As the connection with the other person develops, we move on to physical connections. This includes the way we gently touch someone's arm as we talk, for example, or hug people who are upset.

[Touch is] giving the brain knowledge of me and you, and the emotional quality of gentle, nurturing touch is a very important feeling that underpins a lot of social interaction.

(Denworth, 2015: 32)

Biologically, as relationships develop, these minute connections and interactions tell us we are safe. This then soothes the relevant areas of the brain, the Reticular Activating System (RAS), the nervous system and so on, and means we feel safe with this person. This supports our SEMH and means we can cope with change, uncertainty, and other stresses and challenges of life. Throughout our everyday lives, we send and receive signals to reassure our brains that all is well with the world. A knowing smile or eye contact from someone across the table in a difficult meeting helps us to know we are not alone. The caring voice that asks, 'Are you OK?' Or a gentle touch from a healthcare professional as we prepare for a difficult procedure. All of these types of actions produce a biological reaction, in our brains and nervous systems, they help to lower the hormone cortisol and bring down stress levels. We might still be scared, stressed, or worried – but we know we are not alone. To the human brain – that matters immensely. Lack of relationships and connections (loneliness) also has biological impacts, and the research is very clear:

Loneliness affects 1 million older people …. Loneliness is linked to the onset of dementia … and is associated with depression. It increases as people become less able to undertake routine activities. People who are lonely or isolated are more likely to be admitted to residential or nursing care.

(NICE guideline [NG32], 17 December 2015)

The degree of mortality risk associated with lack of social relationships is similar to that which exists for more widely publicized risk factors, such as smoking.

(Holt-Lunstad et al., 2010: 1)

In other words, relationships, connections, and interactions are good for our physical health, *and* SEMH – *and* the same is true for children. As we mentioned in Chapter 1, in some ways human babies are very underdeveloped at birth. However, there are also some ways that human babies are very advanced, and this is particularly true in terms of making attachments and connections. As Dr Suzanne Zeedyk regularly comments:

> Babies come into the world already connected ... the capacity to be an engaged, relational being doesn't happen sometime later in development, such as when children walk or talk or start school. ... is present from birth. ... matters not from birth but while babies are still in the womb.
>
> (Zeedyk, 2012)

When we are babies, the way adults mirror our facial expressions, respond to the sounds we make, and copy our movements (smiling, cooing, and clapping are good examples here) all send messages to our brains. These, and other similar messages build over time. These messages help build the foundations of self-identity, resilience, and trust, as well as skills around planning and monitoring, for example.

This in turn develops into being able to cope when things are scary. If we think back to Chapter 1, our stress response cannot differentiate between large or small, real or imaginary threats. Our stress responses (fight, flight, freeze and so on) are there to keep us safe – to help us survive. There's some truth in the saying 'safety in numbers' here, our brains are calmed by our relationships. It might help to think about how some animals behave when safety is threatened here. Fish, for example, move about in shoals, changing places constantly to make it harder for predators to pick out individuals for lunch. Several animals, such as elephants, buffalo and dolphins, will create a group with the young hiding in the centre if threatened. For humans, thinking back to our earliest days, children would sleep between adults, as night-time was probably the most dangerous part of the day. In terms of safe food and water, of course our very survival depended on adults.

However, this isn't just about big, scary events, this is also about the everyday challenges of learning to be human. Over time, hopefully, and if we have help from a supportive adult, we learn how to do these things ourselves – and cope when things are difficult, or do not go quite according to plan. For children, this includes things like feeling safe to try a new experience, take on a challenge or take risks. Think how adults respond when babies walk for the first time, try a new food, or a toddler learns to climb or balance on a wall, for example. Or how babies and young children react in new environments/with new people. In addition, think about how adults respond and the messages that we give, when children don't quite succeed at something. Maybe a child has a fall or gets upset or frustrated when trying something new or challenging, or when meeting someone new, or being somewhere different is difficult. Think about what we do to encourage, support and co-regulate. Think about what happens when we use a loving look, an encouraging phrase, an appreciative noise, a reassuring touch?

The Importance of Touch

I have written at great length elsewhere (Garvey, 2018) about the high regard I have for the work of Professor Francis McGlone, Professor in Neuroscience at the School of Natural Sciences and Psychology at Liverpool John Moores University. Prof. McGlone mainly studies the peripheral nerves known as c-fibres (or c-tactile afferents – CTs for short). Recently, Prof. McGlone worked with a team of colleagues (Van Puyvelde et al., 2021), and they offer a warning regarding the impacts of the Covid-19 pandemic:

> Depriving a large part of the world population from social touch (Durkin et al., 2020) … risks to turn our future society into a touch-poor … masked copy of the prior one. It is therefore of extreme importance that we do not forget the crucial impact of touching and being touched.
>
> (Van Puyvelde et al., 2021: 835)

The ECCE sector knew this, and thankfully throughout the Covid-19 pandemic cuddles remained integral to our practice. "Just as plants need water and sunshine, children need a loving and caring environment" (King, 2020 [no page]). The reason I am so invested in Prof. McGlone's and his colleagues work is that they can now prove why cuddles matter. The team used breathing and cortisol testing, and ECG and video imagining to find evidence of how gentle touch is responded to throughout the brain and body. Using the 'still face experiment' (where the carer stops responding to the baby, Tronick et al., 1978), the team measured before and after results. The team of Van Puyvelde, Prof. McGlone and many more (2021) found that babies who had 10 minutes daily optimal stroking from their mothers showed positive differences in heartrate, breathing and cortisol levels, all of which help to regulate the parasympathetic system and stress responses. To me, that is mind-blowing – and something we should be taking very, very, very seriously.

I recognise that not everyone likes hugs and cuddles, and that it is a personal choice (including for children). No one is saying we should be randomly grabbing children and hugging them at every opportunity. But, we do need to be aware of innovative and emerging areas of research and consider how new knowledge impacts on us as adults and children – and particularly on the developing brain. Likewise, we need to consider how we can integrate this into other knowledge we already have on the importance of loving attachments, connections and relationships in early childhood. The evidenced-based research-informed work of Mary Ainsworth, John Bowlby, Professor Sheila Degotardi, Nel Noddings, Dr Jools Page, Dr Suzanne Zeedyk, and many others, would be a good starting point (see bibliography for more). Pauline Scott, Managing Director at Lullaby Lane Nurseries (Tigers Ltd) Glasgow, offers the following reflections on the importance of cuddles:

We Promote Cuddles

At Lullaby Lane Nurseries we place the emotional needs of our children at the heart of our practice. We believe that our children need, and deserve, loving and highly attuned relationships, to develop, thrive and learn. We call our approach Attachment-Led Practice. Our practice and policies are developmentally informed, through our investment in increasing our knowledge of current neuroscience and Attachment Theory.

To support our practice, we have developed a formal partnership with Dr Suzanne Zeedyk, a developmental psychologist and researcher. We have co-designed a training and development programme called 'Daring Ventures', a 12-month programme offered to all our team. The three aims of the programme are to increase our team's confidence and knowledge of Attachment Theory, to translate the theory into practice, and to articulate the knowledge to our children's wider Attachment Community, including parents and families, primary schools, and local authorities.

One of our values is love. We actively promote the importance of providing our children with love. We give permission for our team to develop relationships with our children that allow emotional intimacy, including physical touch. We think this is such an important part of our practice that we have signs above our nursery saying, "we promote cuddles". We know that no significant learning can take place if our children do not feel emotionally safe and secure.

We want our children to feel confident that their keyperson can offer them emotional safety in times of stress or anxiety, in the same way they feel emotionally safe with their primary carers. The science tells us that physical touch is so important to children's emotional and relational development. Cuddles have a significant impact on our hormonal system – and help build connections and trust, between a child and their caregiver. Cuddles are one of the fundamental ways in which we build relationships with our children, to ensure that they feel emotionally safe with their keyperson, prior to parents and family leaving them within our care.

The release of dopamine and serotonin helps us to activate our parasympathetic nervous system, or our "teddy bear system" (Zeedyk, 2013), which is needed to decrease stress, during and after an experience of fear or anxiety. The times that we often observe stress or anxiety within our children is during separation from their families, when they are tired, when they experience conflict with other children, and if they have physically hurt themselves. Offering cuddles allows our team to support our children with their emotions during these experiences and bring their bodies back to a place of calmness and safety. It is in these moments of repetitive co-regulation that our children are building their own self-regulation skills.

We also understand the importance of having emotionally regulated adults present in the lives of our children. To support our team to offer our children co-regulation we have increased awareness of our own stress response systems and our emotional triggers. We have provided our team with techniques and skills to self-regulate to ensure that we have activated our own "teddy bear systems" (Zeedyk, 2013), before we engage with our children. Our team start their day with mindfulness, a breakfast supplied by us, and emotional check-ins. We have also developed a culture that promotes cuddling for the adults too.

Our children at Lullaby Lane can be in our care for up to 50 hours per week. Can you imagine how relationally, emotionally, and physically impoverished our children would be if we did not, or were not allowed to, offer them physical touch and cuddles? For our team at Lullaby Lane, we believe this is not a choice, it is a moral responsibility.

To summarise, as we mentioned previously, Forbes and Gallo (2017: 579) consider love as one of the five elements vital to myelination (faster connections) in the developing brains' "ability to carry out basic motor and cognitive functions". Likewise, babies learn about social communication, turn-taking and timing through watching other faces (Gratier et al., 2015). Connections and relationships bring down stress levels and help with self-regulation skills (see the Center on the Developing Child for example). As for touch, in a 2018 interview, Prof. McGlone stated that "touch is as important as the air we breathe" (see bibliography). All of which are vital to our long-term SEMH.

SEMH, Stress and Self-Regulation

It is fairly clear that relationships and attachments are vital to brain development, and long-term SEMH, and research from a range of sciences is now proving why. We discussed earlier some key influences on our SEMH – specifically in relation to change. Inconsistencies in basic needs, as well as routines and other people's behaviours, all impact on our SEMH – for adults and children. In Chapter 1 we looked at the stress responses; in Chapter 2, we considered the importance of routines, and how key findings from the Covid-19 pandemic identified uncertainty as the biggest detrimental effect on SEMH. Likewise, we've also explored the role of adults in the previous chapter. Here, I just want to touch on why change can make us (as humans) feel stressed, that all-important key message of consistency and the links to SEMH.

REFLECTIVE PRACTICE

SEMH and Stress

Imagine running late for work. Consider the following questions:

How do you feel?
What is happening in your brain?
How is your body reacting?
How do you think this might impact on your SEMH?
Any other thoughts?

As we have discussed throughout this book, previous experiences are vitally important. For this reflective exercise, this could include:

Current workplace and experiences of being late
or seeing the treatment of someone else who was late
Previous workplace experiences of being late
or seeing the treatment of someone else who was late
School/college/university experiences of being late
or seeing the treatment of someone else who was late
Childhood experiences of being late
The messages from communities, cultures, and society about being late

If previous experiences have been positive, or in the community being late is not a big deal, or we are reassured that being late isn't the end of the world – then we will be OK. Our body and brain will be OK too. However, if previous experiences have been difficult, then the likelihood is that the sympathetic nervous system is in 'high alert'. This means many body systems are running faster/higher than normal and the brain is trying desperately to keep the stress responses under control. In other words, previous experiences indicate this is a dangerous situation.

And, I am sure you know the next question... If this is how it feels when we are stressed, then how does it feel for children? (You might want to look again at the reflective practice exercise 'Change vs Consistency' and reconsider how Rahul might feel.)

As we've discussed elsewhere, our brains cannot differentiate whether something is dangerous/life threatening or not. So, our brains/bodies respond as *if* the situation is life threatening and the outcome is that we feel stressed. This is also true for many situations where we feel stressed – not just being late for work. Our responses are based on previous experiences, and the knowledge that we have built from those experiences. Our previous experiences are likely based on:

Intentional reactions/treatment from others
Unintentional reactions/treatment from others
Seeing other peoples' reactions/treatment from others

Most people are not intentionally cruel; however, some people/organisations can, for example, intentionally (and rigidly) follow and enforce policies, procedures and systems which unintentionally cause stress. Likewise, the smallest of acts, deeds or words can be deep and profound. A positive comment, a thank you, or witnessing kindness, for example, can cause unintentional but deep emotional reactions. These might seem so small and insignificant, but these seemingly random acts of kindness can bring untold relief when everything else around all seems just a bit much. And – our brains remember, even if it was a very long time ago. Yes, the person may have acted intentionally – it is our reaction that they did not intend. Plus, the other person might not see our reaction because it happens later, once we are alone, for example.

In terms of our SEMH, it is how we deal with stress that is important. There are many ways humans can deal with stress. The Five Ways to Wellbeing website is a good place to start if you want some ideas to try. For now though, if you think back to the reflective practice exercises and discussions in this chapter, the importance of relationships has been a central thread. In neuroscience terms, relationships help us feel safe and this is particularly true when we feel stressed. Sometimes, our stress levels are so high that we can feel confused, overwhelmed, and disorientated, for example. 'I don't know what to do' or 'I don't know which way to turn' and similar thoughts run through our minds – often, over and over and over again. We might have difficulty concentrating, sleeping can be disturbed and we might not make the healthiest choices for our bodies. This is the RAS doing its job well. It is trying to keep the brain focused on the 'threat' and stop us thinking about anything else. Biologically, the sympathetic nervous system (see Chapters 1 and 2) is in overdrive. If we are struggling to keep the stress levels under control, this means the parasympathetic system might need help to return systems to normal – this is known as co-regulation.

Co-Regulation and Self-Regulation

Yes, there are times when keeping everything under control can be harder. Being worried, or hungry, tired, ill, or too hot, or the behaviours of others, for example, can all have an impact. However, the vast majority of the time, as adults, we can regulate our emotions, systems, and behaviours – in other words, we can self-regulate. Sometimes though, we might need a calm caring 'other' to help us when we feel confused, overwhelmed, and dysregulated. Those times when stress isn't tolerable (Chapter 1). Those times when only a chat (or a cry) with a good listener will do. Again, our experiences and consistency are vital here. If we have had helpful, consistent experiences of other people listening and supporting – then we are more likely to ask for help. Of course, the opposite is also sadly true.

The skills of self-regulation CANNOT BE TAUGHT. I rarely put words in capitals but here it feels needed. There is growing evidence that some level of self-regulation is biological, and there may be gender differences, but this is still in development. What is known, is that the ability to self-regulate is built on consistent relationships over time (Birth to 5 Matters, 2021; Center on the Developing Child, 2022; Veijalainen et al., 2019). And – every human is different, and some find it harder than others, whether children or adults.

As babies and children develop within safe and trusting relationships and environments, adults support children with big emotions and feelings (co-regulate). In turn, this helps to create buffers against long-term implications and lasting impacts. This supports the brain, sympathetic nervous system, and parasympathetic nervous system to begin to understand how to work together. Over time, we learn how to handle emotions, stresses, challenges and so adapt our behaviours appropriately. Sadly, the opposite is also true:

> Stress, especially stress early in life, can have lasting impacts on neural development and behavior. In particular, during peri-adolescence, the prefrontal cortex is still developing and is highly sensitive to stress (Eiland and Romeo, 2013).
>
> (Breton, 2020: 120)

> Exposure to childhood adversity, such as child maltreatment, poverty, and violence exposure, has been associated with poor self-regulation skills (Kim and Cicchetti, 2010; Kim-Spoon et al., 2012; Shipman et al., 2007) and may be a mechanism through which cumulative risk influences children's health, mental health, and well-being.
>
> (Loomis, 2021: 229)

However, we also know that early childhood practitioners can help buffer against adverse and difficult home lives. In other words, what we in early childhood *do* and *how* we do it, matters. The warm, caring relationships, the 'professional love' (Page, 2011, 2014, 2016, 2017; Recchia et al., 2018) for the children and the environments we provide all help – and help significantly (Pascal and Bertram, 2016; Shonkoff and Philips, 2000).

I am going to resist the urge to put in a reflective practice exercise here. There are others, both in this chapter and elsewhere that will work in just the same way – and lead to the same conclusions:

> What do other people do that make us feel supported and listened to?
> How do we feel when we are not supported and listened to?
> How do we feel when someone we trust, listens and is supportive?
>> How do all of these influence our stress levels, behaviours and so on?
>> What else can impact on our stress levels, behaviours and so on?

And of course, the usual reflection:

> If this is how it feels for adults – how does it feel for children?

There is one final piece I think is worth mentioning here. The area of the brain responsible for being able to manage our own emotions, behaviours and self-regulation, is one of the last to mature – often extending into adolescence, and even adulthood. When I read that last sentence back it strikes me as odd that we expect our very youngest children to be able to do something that their brain is perhaps not fully capable of until early adulthood. And no, I am not saying that children should behave in any way they see fit. Quite the opposite in fact. What I am saying is that we need to remember that being able to self-regulate takes time – and can be difficult, even for adults. I am going to leave the final quote to Dr Maria Montessori (1912: 98, *emphasis in original*):

> We do not stop to think that the child *who does not do,*
> *does not know how to do.*

Chapter Reflection

Thinking back over this chapter, consider the various elements (sections, quotes, reflective exercises, terminology, etc.). Are there any elements that:

Were particularly useful?
Need re-reading, or more thought or reflection?
You want to look up and/or explore further?

Any other thoughts or reflections?

Bibliography

The following are books, articles, web pages, organisations, documents, etc. that I have found useful (online versions, all accessed 20 July 2022). Some are directly referenced in this chapter – some are included as valuable sources of background reading that might be helpful. See also web resources at the end of Chapter 1.

Ainsworth, M. D. S. and Bell, S. M. (1970) Attachment, exploration, and separation: illustrated by the behaviour of one-year-olds in a strange situation. *Journal of Child Development*, 41, pp. 49–67. Available at: https://doi.org/10.2307/1127388.

Ainsworth, M. D. S., Blehar, M. C., Waters, E. and Wall, S. (1978) *Patterns of Attachment: A Psychological Study of the Strange Situation*. Hillsdale, NJ: Erlbaum.

Ainsworth, M. I. S. and Wittig, B. A. (1969) Attachment and the exploratory behaviour of one-year-olds in a strange situation. In: B. M. Foss, ed. *Determinants of Infant Behaviour*. London: Methuen, pp. 113–136.

Barnardo's Northern Ireland (2018) *Promoting Good Infant Mental Health: Supporting Emotional Wellbeing for 0–3 Year Olds*. [pdf] Belfast: Barnardo's. Available at: https://www.barnardos.org.uk/sites/default/files/uploads/Information%20for%20Parents%20booklet.pdf.

Bowlby, J. (1953) *Child Care and the Growth of Love*. Middlesex: Penguin.

Bowlby, J. (1969) *Attachment and Loss: Volume 1. Attachment*. New York: Basic Books.

Bowlby, J. (1973) *Attachment and Loss: Volume 2. Separation: Anxiety and Anger*. New York: Basic Books.

Bowlby, J. (1988) *A Secure Base: Parent-Child Attachment and Healthy Human Development*. New York: Basic Books.

Breton, J. (2020) *The Role of the Prefrontal Cortex in Stress and Motivation* (Doctoral dissertation, UC Berkeley).

Campaign to End Loneliness (2022) Available at: https://www.campaigntoendloneliness.org/.

Degotardi, S. and Pearson. E. (2009) Relationship theory in the nursery: attachment and beyond. *Contemporary Issues in Early Childhood* 10(2), pp. 144–155. Available at: https://doi.org/10.2304%2Fciec.2009.10.2.144.

Denworth, L. (2015) The social power of touch. *Scientific American Mind*, 26, pp. 30–39. Available at: https://www.scientificamerican

.com/article/touch-s-social-significance-could-be-explained-by
-unique-nerve-fibers/#:~:text=Full%20of%20Feeling,role%20in
%20reinforcing%20social%20connections.

Durkin, J., Jackson, D. and Usher, K. (2020) Touch in times of COVID19: touch hunger hurts. *Journal of Clinical Nursing*, 30(1–2), pp. e4–e5. Available at: https://onlinelibrary.wiley.com/doi/10.1111/jocn.15488.

Eiland, L. and Romeo, R. D. (2013) Stress and the developing adolescent brain. *Neuroscience*, 249, pp. 162–171. Available at: https://doi.org /10.1016/j.neuroscience.2012.10.048.

Elfer, P. (2006) Exploring children's expressions of attachment in nursery. *European Early Childhood Education Research Journal*, 14(2), pp. 81–95. Available at: https://doi.org/10.1080 /13502930285209931.

Faulkner (2022) Heatwave: National emergency declared after U.K.'s first red extreme heat warning. *BBC News*, 15 July. Available at: https://www.bbc.co.uk/news/uk-62177458.

Five Ways to Wellbeing:

Report: Aked, J., Marks, N., Cordon, C. and Thompson, S. (2008) *Five Ways to Wellbeing*. [pdf] London: New Economics Foundation. Available at: https://neweconomics.org/2008/10/five-ways-to -wellbeing.

Forbes, T. A. and Gallo, V. (2017) All wrapped up: environmental effects on myelination. *Trends in neurosciences*, 40(9), pp. 572–587. Available at: https://doi.org/10.1016/j.tins.2017.06.009.

Garvey, D. (2018) *Nurturing Personal, Social and Emotional Development in Early Childhood: A Practical Guide to Understanding Brain Development and Young Children's Behaviour*. London: Jessica Kingsley Publishers.

Gopnik, A. (2010) *The Philosophical Baby: What Children's Minds Tell Us About Truth, Love, and the Meaning of Life*. New York: Farrar, Straus and Giroux.

Goswami, U. (2020) *Cognitive Development and Cognitive Neuroscience: The Learning Brain.* 2nd edn. Abingdon: Routledge.

Gratier, M., Devouche, E., Guellai, B., Infanti, R., Yilmaz, E. and Parlato-Oliveira, E. (2015) Early development of turn-taking in vocal interaction between mothers and infants. *Frontiers in Psychology,* 6(1167), pp. 1–10. Available at: https://doi.org/10.3389/fpsyg.2015.01167.

Grimmer, T. (2021) *Developing a Loving Pedagogy in the Early Years: How Love Fits with Professional Practice.* Abingdon: Routledge.

Holt-Lunstad, J., Smith, T. B. and Layton, J. B., (2010) Social relationships and mortality risk: a meta-analytic review. *PLoS medicine,* 7(8), pp. 1–2. Available at: https://doi.org/10.1371/journal.pmed.1000316.

Kim, J. and Cicchetti, D. (2010) Longitudinal pathways linking child maltreatment, emotion regulation, peer relations, and psychopathology. *Journal of Child Psychology and Psychiatry,* 51(6), pp. 706–716. Available at: https://doi.org/10.1111/j.1469-7610.2009.02202.x.

Kim-Spoon, J., Haskett, M. E., Longo, G. S. and Nice, R. (2012) Longitudinal study of self-regulation, positive parenting, and adjustment problems among physically abused children. *Child Abuse and Neglect,* 36(2), pp. 95–107. Available at: https://doi.org/10.1016/j.chiabu.2011.09.016.

King, S. (2020) 'Kids need contact': nursery staff during lockdown – a photo essay. *The Guardian,* 10 August. Available at: https://www.theguardian.com/education/2020/aug/10/kids-need-contact-nursery-staff-during-lockdown-a-photo-essay.

Loomis, A. M. (2021) Effects of household and environmental adversity on indices of self-regulation for Latino and African American preschool children: closing the school readiness gap. *Early Education and Development,* 32(2), pp. 228–248. Available at: https://doi.org/10.1080/10409289.2020.1745513.

Mainstone-Cotton, S. (2021) *Supporting Children with Social, Emotional and Mental Health Needs in the Early Years: Practical Solutions and Strategies for Every Setting.* Abingdon: Routledge.

Marmot, M. (2016) *The Health Gap: The Challenge of an Unequal World*. London: Bloomsbury.

National Institute for Health and Care Excellence (NICE)

National Institute for Health and Care Excellence (2015a) *Excess Winter Deaths and Illness and the Health Risks Associated with Cold Homes* (NICE Guideline 6). Available at: https://www.nice .org.uk/guidance/ng6/chapter/What-is-this-guideline-about.
National Institute for Health and Care Excellence (2015b) *Nutrition Support in Adults* (NICE Quality Standard 24). Available at: https:// www.nice.org.uk/guidance/qs24.
National Institute for Health and Care Excellence (2015c) *Older People: Independence and Mental Wellbeing* (NICE Guideline 32). Available at: https://www.nice.org.uk/guidance/ng32.
National Institute for Health and Care Excellence (2015d) *Preventing Excess Weight Gain* (NICE Guideline 7). Available at: https://www.nice.org.uk/guidance/ng7/chapter/What-is-this -guideline-about.
National Institute for Health and Care Excellence (2022a) *Health topics: Insomnia*. Available at: https://cks.nice.org.uk/topics/ insomnia/.
National Institute for Health and Care Excellence (2022b) *Overview*. Available at: https://www.nice.org.uk/about/what-we -do.

Noddings, N. (1984) *Caring: A Feminine Approach to Ethics and Moral Education*. Berkeley, CA: University of California Press.
OECD (Organisation for Economic Co-operation and Development) (2002) *Understanding the Brain: Towards a New Learning Science*. Paris: OECD Publishing.
Pascal, C. and Bertram, T. (2016) *High Achieving White Working Class (HAWWC) Boys Project: Final Report*. [website] Birmingham: CREC (Centre for Research in Early Childhood). Available at: https://www .crec.co.uk/hawwc-boys.

Page, J. (2011) Do mothers want professional carers to love their babies? *Journal of Early Childhood Research*, 9(3), pp. 310–323. Available at: https://doi.org/10.1177/1476718X11407980.

Page, J. (2014) Developing professional love in early childhood settings. In: L. Harrison and J. Sumsion, eds. *International Perspectives on Early Childhood and Development: Lived Spaces of Infant-Toddler Education and Care: Exploring Diverse Perspectives on Theory, Research and Practice*. Dordrecht, NL: Springer, pp. 119–130.

Page, J. (2016) Educators' perspectives on attachment and professional love in early years settings in England. In: E. J. White and C. Dalli, eds. *Under Three-Year-Olds in Policy and Practice: Policy and Pedagogy with Under-Three-Year-Olds: Cross-Disciplinary Insights and Innovations for Educational Research with Very Young Children Series*. Dordrecht, NL: Springer, pp. 131–142.

Page, J. (2017) Reframing infant-toddler pedagogy through a lens of professional love: exploring narratives of professional practice in early childhood settings in England. *Contemporary Issues in Early Childhood*, 18(4), pp. 387–399. Available at: https://doi.org/10.1177/1463949117742780.

Professor Francis McGlone

Liverpool John Moore University. Available at: https://www.ljmu.ac.uk/about-us/staff-profiles/faculty-of-health/school-of-psychology/francis-mcglone.

Play Therapy U.K. Conference (2018) The neuroscience of touch: An interview with Professor Francis McGlone. *PTUK, 25 September*, Beaumont Estate, Windsor. [video] Available at: https://www.youtube.com/watch?v=oG9ZxfD6U90.

Blume, A. (2017) Exclusive: Refusing to touch pupils is a form of child abuse, psychologists say. *Times Educational Supplement*, 17 February. Available at: https://www.tes.com/magazine/archive/exclusive-refusing-touch-pupils-form-child-abuse-psychologists-say.

Recchia, S. L., Shin, M. and Snaider, C. (2018) Where is the love? Developing loving relationships as an essential component of professional infant care. *International Journal of Early Years Education*, 26(2), pp. 142–158. Available at: https://doi.org/10.1080/09669760.2018.1461614.

Sartorius, N. (2006) The meanings of health and its promotion. *Croatian Medical Journal*, 47(4), pp. 662–664. Available at: https://www.ncbi.nlm.nih.gov/pmc/articles/PMC2080455/.

Shipman, K. L., Medical, C., Fitzgerald, M. M., Carolina, S., Sims, C. and Edwards, A. (2007) Maternal emotion socialization in maltreating and non-maltreating families: Implications for children's emotion regulation. *Social Development*, 16(2), pp. 268–285. Available at: https://doi.org/10.1111/j.1467-9507.2007.00384.x.

Shonkoff, J. P. and Phillips, D. A. eds. (2000) *From Neurons to Neighborhoods: The Science of Early Childhood Development.* Washington, DC: National Academy Press.

Tronick, E., Als, H., Adamson, L., Wise, S. and Brazelton, T. B. (1978) The infant's response to entrapment between contradictory messages in face-to-face interaction. *Journal of the American Academy of Child Psychiatry*, 17(1), pp. 1–13. Available at: https://doi.org/10.1016/S0002-7138(09)62273-1.

World Health Organisation (2018) *Mental Health: Strengthening Our Response.* Available at: https://www.who.int/news-room/fact-sheets/detail/mental-health-strengthening-our-response.

Van Puyvelde, M., Staring, L., Schaffers, J., Rivas-Smits, C., Groenendijk, L., Smeyers, L., Collette, L., Schoofs, A., Van den Bossche, N. and McGlone, F. P. (2021) Why do we hunger for touch? The impact of daily gentle touch stimulation on maternal-infant physiological and behavioral regulation and resilience. *Infant Mental Health Journal*, 42(6), pp. 823–883. Available at: https://doi.org/10.1002/imhj.21949.

Veijalainen, J., Reunamo, J. and Heikkilä, M. (2019) Early gender differences in emotional expressions and self-regulation in settings of early childhood education and care. *Early Child Development*

and *Care*, 191(2), pp. 173–186. Available at: https://doi.org/10.1080
/03004430.2019.1611045.

Zeedyk, S. (1994) *Disconnection and the Still Face Paradigm* [video].
Available at: https://www.youtube.com/watch?v=LJRVKcOZrmU.

Zeedyk, S. (2012) *Babies Come into the World Already Connected to
Other People*. Dundee: Suzanne Zeedyk Ltd. Available at: https://
www.suzannezeedyk.com/wp-content/uploads/2016/03/Suzanne
-Zeedyk-Babies-Connected-v2.pdf.

Zeedyk, S. (2013) *Sabre Tooth Tigers and Teddy Bears: The Connected
Baby Guide to Understanding Attachment*. Dundee: Suzanne
Zeedyk Ltd.

This is a book about neuroscience and brain development. It is also a book about early childhood. But, my dear reader, it is also a book about you! After all, we cannot support children's brains if we don't look after our own! Throughout the book we have seen the golden thread of the importance of adults and our influences on early childhood development. We have also discussed how the growing scientific evidence on how brains work is about human development and applies to adults, as well as children. Even some of the reflective exercises are about thinking how we react as adults. This chapter will bring all of this together and consider how we can use reflective practice to help. This is not as long a chapter as the others – but there are very good reasons for *why* this chapter is included here at the end of *this* book.

As you have probably realised by reading this book, I am a big fan of reflective practice. In addition, people tell me that the reflective exercises are one of the things they like most about my books. I'll come back to the *why* a little later, but let's start with the *what*, and a short exploration on some reflective practice theory. (As always, check the bibliography for more.)

What Is Reflection?

Of course, the most common meaning of reflection is associated with mirrors:

> If we take this as a literal meaning, what do we see when we look in the mirror? Obvious – we see ourselves.
>
> (Garvey and Lancaster, 2010: 26)

DOI: 10.4324/9781003154846-7

This is a useful starting point for a discussion about reflection – reflection is looking at ourselves. The key here is *how* we look at ourselves:

> Gazing into a mirror can be a rather superficial activity. … the image can be distorted and we may even choose to look at ourselves from a flattering angle.
>
> (Garvey and Lancaster, 2010: 27)

> It may be that we can develop this idea further. Think about a fairground hall of mirrors where the image we see of ourselves is distorted. Now consider your own reflection in your own mirror – is that not distorted too? When we look in the mirror a host of issues can interfere with the image we see, for example, health concerns, feelings, insecurities, emotions or past experiences. … you could have a very distorted view of your own traits and qualities.
>
> (Garvey and Lancaster, 2010: 25)

As these few quotes show, reflection is potentially an emotive, subjective, and possibly a biased activity. In addition, reflection can be personal or in a group, it can be thinking, talking, drawing, writing. Reflection can be over a period of time, or in a moment. Reflection *should not* be a one-off event, used only for difficult or negative experiences, used as a punishment, taken out of context, or seen as a magic wand. In other words, reflection *should* be a supportive, ongoing process, used to consider contexts, what is going well and what needs further development, as part of an ongoing approach to Continuous Professional Development (CPD). Similarly, reflective practice can also be helpful to personal development. I would actually go further and say – reflective practice is (or *should* be) part of *human* development.

Developing Reflective Practice

One of the questions I get asked most about reflection is – *how* to do it. My answer is always that there is no right or wrong way – it is about what works for you. You can just start jotting down thoughts if that works for you. Likewise, if having pointers helps, there is a huge amount of research behind reflection, and we can use this to develop our practice. (See bibliography for more.) In my experience, when considering reflection (or indeed starting to reflect) it can be useful to have a bit of a starting point. Whether we are new, or experienced, anxious, or eager, as reflective practitioners having a model, framework or template can be a helpful way to guide our thinking. A quick internet search will bring up hundreds (if not thousands) of reflection models, frameworks, and templates. Works by Borton (1970), Driscoll (1994, 2000), Gibbs (1988) and Rolfe et al. (2001) have been developed and interpreted by multiple authors over time. Most models are based on a series of questions, some are more complex than others. The grid in the following reflective practice exercise is an amalgamation of some key reflective questions.

REFLECTIVE PRACTICE
Using a Questioning Model to Support Reflection

Most reflection models ask us to consider a particular situation or event and use questions to help us explore our thinking. Therefore, think about a situation you have been involved in recently. You don't have to think about a 'big, scary' stressful situation, unless of course you want to. Just a straightforward, 'normal' event that caused you to think about it afterwards – maybe an interaction with a colleague, a meeting, or an interview perhaps.

The questions here are just examples, ideas to start the thinking process. Use the ones that are useful, or adapt or change them to suit your particular needs. Likewise, there is not a blank grid to fill in with this exercise. *How* you do this, is a personal decision. Reflection should not be prescriptive – by all means copy a similar grid if that would be helpful. Or you could use a spidergram, a word cloud, you could draw, do a vlog, talk it through with a trusted colleague, or just simply write – whatever works for you. Also, feel free to try out a few of these different ways – different situations often need different types of reflection.

A Questioning Model to Support Reflection			
What?	Description	This is the description of our personal knowledge and understanding of the situation.	What happened/is happening? What did I do? What did other people do? What was I trying to achieve? What was good/bad or helpful/unhelpful about the experience?
So What?	Feelings Evaluation Analysis	A deeper exploration of what was behind the experience.	So what is the importance of this? So what does my thinking tell me? So what reasons could there be/is there more I need to find out? So what do I/others feel about this? So what do I now understand/ have I learnt? So what could/should I (or others) have done differently? So what are the implications?
Now what?	Conclusion Action Plan	Think about and consider, what we could do next.	Now what could/might/should I do? Now what could/might be the consequences? Now what could/might I do differently next time? Now what do I need to do next (action plan)? Now what is my first step?

As with any model, there are limitations to how useful it can be, and you may well have changed or developed the questions to suit your own style of reflection. That is one of the great things about reflection – it can be tweaked to suit individual needs and situations. With this model, there is also the option to add an additional layer.

What Now?	Afterthoughts	What are your thoughts and feelings now? So what difference has some time made? Now what are your thoughts?	The idea behind this layer is (if you want to) to reconsider the situation when some time has passed. It could be a few days/weeks/months – it is up to you. It can be a useful exercise especially with a reflection that has been emotive.

In terms of the optional final layer in the 'Questioning Model to Support Reflection', it is worth bearing in mind that our reflections can change over time. This links to our earlier discussions around Bronfenbrenner's ecological model (1979, 1992; Bronfenbrenner and Ceci, 1994, for example), and the 'chronosystem' influences of time, experience, learning, change, and so on. In addition, how we reflect depends on the other things that are going on around us at that moment in time. The likelihood is that if we considered the same event in, say, six months' or five years' time, our reflections would be very different. This in itself, can be a useful reflection – how does time influence our thinking? Hopefully, this exercise has given you a flavour of how using reflection models can help our thinking and, perhaps, how they can be used to support reflection in the workplace.

Reflection in the Workplace

Reflective practice *should* have a central role in the workplace. Note, the word 'should'. In reality, reflection can get lost in the busyness of the day and become something that only happens when things go wrong. For me, reflection should be central to CPD, and central to a positive performance management model (Garvey, 2017: 116, *emphasis in original*):

CPD is, and should be, anything and everything associated with a role. CPD is about *continuing* (or continuous) *professional development*. Therefore, virtually every and any activity linked to a role could be classed as CPD. Effective induction, on-the-job support, keeping a journal, mentoring, peer observation, training, supervision, etc. all offer valuable opportunities to support the ongoing development of a professional practitioner.

In other words, CPD should be about offering positive performance management opportunities and supporting all staff to succeed in their roles. And therefore, all of these activities can and should be linked to opportunities for reflection. In my book *Performance Management in Early Years Settings* (Garvey, 2017), we looked at the role of CPD across a range of job-related activities, to support positive performance management opportunities. Here, let's explore how job-related activities could support reflection and therefore develop practice.

REFLECTIVE PRACTICE

Opportunities for Reflection

Consider the grid. In the first column are some job-related activities that offer potential opportunities to support reflection, and to develop reflective practice skills. Some will perhaps be well established; others may need further consideration.

The second column has some questions that might help your reflections – use the ones that are useful, ignore some – and add your own. Make the reflection opportunity work for you.

For all of the questions, also consider:

How do you know?
Why do you think that?

The third column is for you to jot down your thoughts and comments.
There are no right or wrong answers – it is the reflection that is important.

Opportunities for Reflective Practice Development

Opportunities for Reflective Practice Development		
Job-Related Activities	Opportunities for Reflection	Thoughts and Comments
Recruitment and selection process	How are *all* staff and practitioners included and involved? (Existing and new.)	
Staff handbook		
Induction	How is reflection embedded in this area/activity?	
Training (formal and informal)	How is learning from reflection shared with others/across the team?	
Journaling		
Team meetings		
Peer observation	Who could help/support?	
Mentoring/coaching		
Supervision/one-to-one	When are staff/practitioners able to reflect?	
Monitoring paperwork (sickness and so on)	What works well?	
Other job-related paperwork	What needs further development?	
Appraisal	What difference does this make to children, families, staff, communities, etc.?	
	Anything else?	

Supporting and actively offering reflection opportunities will generate a wealth of information, knowledge, and data. In other words, evidence. Reflection opportunities provide valuable evidence for both practitioners and leaders. On one hand there will be clear evidence of what is working well, and on the other, clear evidence of what needs further development. This gives both practitioners and leaders a solid foundation on which to build.

Ultimately, reflective practice has to work for the person doing it – there is no right or wrong way. However, there are a couple of key elements: it has to be genuine, and it has to have allocated time. In other words, we have to want to reflect and consider things on a deeper level and be prepared for what reflection might uncover. Schön (1983) talked of reflection in action (at the time/in the moment) and reflection on action (later, or after the event). In my experience, reflection can be just a few connected thoughts, and some-times that is all that is needed – a true 'lightbulb' moment. But sometimes, we need to really think carefully about something.

Therefore, we need to recognise the value of allowing ourselves time to think and reflect. Usually, the things we need to take time to think about are the things that need deeper, critical (significant) and thoughtful reflection. This could be something we are worried about, or something that we are not happy with, often it can be something that needs to change. Usually, it is the very things that keep us awake at night. Which brings us to the 'why' of reflection.

I have regularly written about the 'what' and the 'how' of reflective practice, but never really written about why I am such a huge advocate for reflective practice – until now. Why do I find reflective practice so useful? Why do I think it should be a standard part of our work in the sector? ..... In my experience, having opportunity to pause and reflect is an extremely valuable use of time. Reflection offers an opportunity to think about the 'what, how, where, when, who and why' we do what we do. For example, reflection ensures we hear children's voices and reminds us 'why' we do what we do and helps us to consider 'how' we do it. Reflection encourages us to think about 'who' else we could talk to, and 'what' else could help. Reflection helps us to think about our next steps and the 'where' and 'when'.

Reflection can be emotional, intense, painful, messy but equally cathar-tic, healing, and enlightening. And, in terms of this book, reflection is helpful to the human brain – and that is why this chapter is included at the end of this book.

The Neuroscience Behind Reflective Practice

As we have discussed elsewhere, the human brain cannot differentiate between a real threat and a perceived one. In other words, our brains worry (intensely sometimes) about things that might, could or perhaps will happen. Or we spend a huge amount of time worrying about our perceptions, and what we think other people are thinking and feeling. In neuroscience terms, our cortisol and adrenaline levels rise, our stress responses are activated, our systems run faster, and we *cannot* think straight. As Daniel Goleman (1996: 149), clearly explains:

> When emotionally upset, people cannot remember, attend, learn, or make decisions clearly.

Reflective practice can help! I know this is a big statement – but I'll say it again – reflective practice can help. Nagoski and Nagoski in their book *Burnout* (2020: 14–21) consider how often, when having experienced a stressful situation, we do not have the opportunity to complete the stress cycle. In other words – we are off on to the next thing, and the stress remains floating around in our bodies unsure of where to go next.

If we think about times when we have been stressed, I am sure we can all probably think of those occasions when our shoulders ache, or we wake in the middle of the night worrying about something. This is our body's way of telling us that the stress has not been fully dealt with. It is a biological response. It is the brain and central nervous system telling us that the para-sympathetic nervous system cannot do its job and bring everything back to normal levels. In addition, if we then experience more stressful events (real or perceived), we can have numerous unfinished stress cycles. It is no wonder the reptilian brain and Reticular Activating System (RAS) filter want us to scream and shout – or run and hide. (See Chapter 1.)

Nagoski and Nagoski (2020) talk of ways to complete the stress cycle:

Exercise (at least 20 mins)
Breathing Exercises
Positive Social Interaction
Laughter

Affection
A 'Good' Cry
Creative Expression

So where does reflective practice fit in with this list? Well, for me, I think the activities on this list are often part of reflection. And – I think we should consider how these could further support workplace reflection (there's no reason why we couldn't do a reflective walk, for example). Similarly, when we are stressed, we breathe differently – so learning to breathe deeper and slower helps. I am sure we have all experienced that 'letting out a big breath' moment after coming out of an interview, for example.

Likewise, how much better do we feel when we have had a chance to talk through a situation with a supportive listener. Or how having a good laugh often helps us feel better. Opportunities for interactions, affection and using our skills also helps us to feel valued, provides a sense of belonging and, again, we feel better. As for a good cry – I am not suggesting we make people cry, but I am saying we should understand the importance of tears. Personally, I love walking, and that definitely helps with my stress levels, but I also love a good old black-and-white movie, a bag of popcorn and a box of tissues. I know how therapeutic it is for me, and I understand *why* it helps.

All of the activities in the bullet point list help to calm our biological responses to stress. Therefore, they could potentially all be a wider part of reflective practice opportunities. Let's explore this a little:

REFLECTIVE PRACTICE

Supervision Support

Imagine the following scenario:
    Nathanial is the manager of a small team. Nathanial is well liked, and considered fair, approachable, and keen to support the team. Hélène is a practitioner. Hélène has been with the team for 18 months, and is keen to learn and develop, and is hoping to progress into a management position within the next couple of years.
    They are about to have a discussion as part of Hélène's supervision meeting.

Now consider the following:

Learning to control breathing brings down the heartrate and lowers stress-related hormones.

Positive interactions tell the nervous system we are safe and supports the release of hormones such as oxytocin – which helps to neutralise the effects of stress-related hormones.

Laughter also releases oxytocin. Having the opportunity to share some of the hilarious moments in a working day can be beneficial.

Affection means friendliness, warmth, and kindness, as well as hugs and touch – all of which lower breathing, heartrates and the stress-related hormones. Affection also raises hormones that help.

Tears release cortisol. For example, science can now measure cortisol levels in babies' tears. It is *how* we respond to tears that matters. Having the opportunity for expression shows us we are valued. Feeling valued supports our emotional state, commitment to the team/role, etc., and increases feelings of wellbeing.

What thoughts occur to you reading this?

How could knowing some of this help Nathaniel and Hélène?

How could knowing some of this help us in our day-to-day practice?

Any other thoughts?

Whilst there could be difficult elements that need discussion, overall, supervision should be a supportive and positive interaction. That is not to say we should avoid difficult conversations – in fact I wrote a whole book on it (Garvey, 2017). This is about having those difficult conversations with an awareness of the biology behind our reactions. The discussions here, and elsewhere in this book, link directly to the fight, flight, freeze, etc., responses.

Considering how to deal with the stress cycle offers some clear clues as to how we can help in potentially difficult situations.

Some thoughts to consider:

How do we make sure that the people we are working with are enabled to engage in a way that uses the latest neuroscience research?
How do we ensure that we see the responses to stress as biological – and use our knowledge of biology to support?

(By the way, this works for children too – this is about all humans.)

I am not saying that all of these ways to deal with the stress cycle will be suitable for every one-to-one supervision or meeting, but there are certainly elements we can consider for most occasions. Sometimes it is about being brave and having a go. And that goes for other areas of reflective practice too.

Practitioners as Researchers

I just wanted to explore one last area of reflective practice – the idea of practitioners as researchers. We touched on this briefly in the chapter on behaviours and discussed how we should celebrate our contributions to research, no matter how small. Every adult who spends thoughtful time interacting with young children is potentially a researcher. We watch, think, make suggestions, ask questions, make decisions, and consider what next. Maybe we speak to (or disagree) with another adult about our thoughts. Maybe we read up on something of interest or find out more about a new area. Maybe we note our thoughts down. To put it another way – we observe, consider, reflect, record, recommend, analyse, investigate, examine, theorise, evaluate, evidence, plan, assess, envision, develop.... Do I need to go on? We might not use all of this language – but I would suggest that when we carefully consider our practice, it is a form of practitioner research.

Many of those with an interest in child development will also go on to become researchers in the field.

(Keenan et al., 2016: xxiv)

One of the key elements of research is considering links to seminal (influential) and contemporary (current) theory. Perhaps it would be useful for more opportunities for this to happen in daily practice in order to support reflection. If we reconsidered the 'Opportunities for Reflection' exercise, it could so easily be modified to support opportunities for research. From the moment we are considering recruiting, research can help. For example, does the job description discuss keeping up to date with current thinking? How can CPD, team meetings, supervision, and appraisals, etc., offer opportunity to consider influential/the latest thinking? Are policies, procedures, planning, and practices linked to evidence-based, research-informed theory? And for all of these questions…. If not, why not?

Throughout this book, there have been opportunities to pause and think about what we do and why, using seminal and contemporary research, theory, quotes and references to help. Some quotes will be very familiar, some perhaps new – some may have even caused debate. Hopefully, all offered opportunity for careful, considered, thinking and reflection. As we explored elsewhere, research from a range of other fields and writers can help too:

> The boundaries that define the field of child development are becoming increasingly blurred.
>
> (Hopkins et al., 2017: xxvii)

Using evidence-based, research-informed theory from a range of areas can support and develop practitioner research and ensure our practice is appropriate. In addition, sometimes the importance of early childhood can feel unappreciated, unrecognised, and undervalued (Beltman et al., 2020; Hardy et al., 2022), and there are times when we have to defend our philosophies, principles, and practices. Being aware of the research, widening our reading and having conversations with like-minded professionals can help bring confidence to these debates (Archer, 2021; Sims, 2017), and empower us to do what is right for children. Therefore, keeping up to date and open minded in relation to what might be developing in the sector and elsewhere is vital to the early childhood profession.

Finding My 'Why'

I never intended to be a researcher (or write books for that matter). I have always worked with families and communities, colleagues and teams, with children at the heart of practice. I came into early childhood, as I suspect many of you did, to make a difference to children's lives. That is still the case. I write books to (hopefully) share some thoughts and ideas that make lives better for more children, their families and communities, and the wonderful practitioners, like you, who make a difference every day. I also believe in the saying 'you are never too old to learn', and now find myself in my mid-50s (and the first person in my family) undertaking my MA. And this is another reason this chapter is here at the end of this book – the MA has reminded me how important reflection and practitioner research is. We owe it to ourselves to do the things that bring us joy and fulfilment – equally we owe it to children to ensure that we know *why* we do what we do! And, so one final reflection opportunity – looking at developing research within, and for, and with, the early childhood sector.

REFLECTIVE EXERCISE

Practitioner Reflection: Case Study

You might have noticed that there is no case study in this chapter. That is because it is now over to *you*. This is *your* case study.

Consider your journey through this book. Where have your thinking and reflections taken you? Where will you go next?

Have a look at the subjects in the grid. Included are a wide range of topics that either I am currently researching, or we have covered, or that could be useful to support reflection and practice in the early childhood sector. This reflective exercise is a challenge – from me to you. As I move forward, I will share with the sector the things I find out – please would you do the same? Pick one category and find out a little about it, reflect on it, try it out in your practice, consider the difference knowing about the subject makes to children, families, colleagues, and the sector. In other words, write your own case study. And – let me know how you get on – I would love to know where your research and your reflections take you!

(The categories are in no particular order, and you will see there are a few blank boxes for you to add in your own areas of research interest.)

Brain Development	Environments	Professional Love	Impact of Hormones
Diversity & Inclusion		Self-Regulation	Political Influences
Praxis & Praxeology (1)	Social, Emotional & Mental Health	Behaviours	
Play	Anthropology		Special Educational Needs & Disability
	Sustained Shared Thinking	Serve & Return	Neoliberalism (2)
Continuous Provision – EY	Continuous Provision – School	Stress	
Reflective Practice		Bronfenbrenner	Imposter Syndrome
	Ethnography & Autoethnography (3)	Women's Health	Feedback
Resilience	Leadership in Early Childhood		Poverty

All the categories are mentioned in bibliographies throughout the book; (1), (2) and (3) are in the bibliography at the end of this chapter.

Final Reflections

Thinking back over this book, consider the various chapters, sections, quotes, reflective exercises, terminology, etc. Are there any elements that:

Were particularly useful?
Need re-reading, or more thought or reflection?
You want to look up and/or explore further?

Any other thoughts or reflections?

Bibliography

The following are books, articles, web pages, organisations, documents, etc. that I have found useful (online versions, all accessed 20 July 2022). Some are directly referenced in this chapter – some are included as valuable sources of background reading that might be helpful. See also web resources at the end of Chapter 1.

Archer, N. (2021) I have this subversive curriculum underneath: narratives of micro resistance in early childhood education. *Journal of Early Childhood Research*, 20(3), pp. 431–445. Available at: https://doi.org/10.1177/1476718X211059907.

Archer, N. and Albin-Clark, J. (2022) Telling stories that need telling a dialogue on resistance in early childhood education. *FORUM*, 64(2), pp. 21–29.

Beltman, S., Dobson, M. R., Mansfield, C. F. and Jay, J. (2020) The thing that keeps me going: educator resilience in early learning settings. *International Journal of Early Years Education*, 28(4), pp. 303–318. https://doi.org/10.1080/09669760.2019.1605885.

Borton, T. (1970) *Reach, Touch and Teach*. New York: McGraw-Hill Paperbacks.

Bronfenbrenner, U. (1979) *The Ecology of Human Development: Experiments by nature and design*. Cambridge, MA: Harvard University Press.

Bronfenbrenner, U. (1986) Ecology of the family as a context for human development. *Developmental Psychology*, 22(6), pp. 723–742. Available at: https://psycnet.apa.org/doi/10.1037/0012-1649.22.6.723.

Bronfenbrenner, U. (1992) *Ecological Systems Theory*. London: Jessica Kingsley Publishers.

Bronfenbrenner, U. and Ceci, S. J. (1994) Nature-nurture reconceptualized in developmental perspective: a bioecological model. *Psychological Review*, 101, pp. 568–586. Available at: https://doi.org/10.1037/0033-295x.101.4.568.

Brookfield, S. (2005) *Becoming a Critically Reflective Teacher*. San Francisco, CA: Jossey Bass.

Driscoll, J. (1994) Reflective practice for practise – a framework of structured reflection for clinical areas. *Senior Nurse*, 14(1), pp. 47–50.

Driscoll, J. (2000) *Practising Clinical Supervision: A Reflective Approach*. London: Bailliere Tindall (in association with the Royal College of Nursing).

Fairchild, N. and Kay, L. (2020) The early years foundation stage (2021): challenges and opportunities. *BERA (British Education Research Association)*. [blog] 26 November. Available at: https://www.bera .ac.uk/blog/the-early-years-foundation-stage-2021-challenges-and -opportunities.

Fisher, N. (2020) Schools out. *The British Psychological Society*. [blog] 03 February. Available at: https://www.bps.org.uk/psychologist/ schools-out.

Garvey, D. (2017) *Performance Management in Early Years Settings: A Practical Guide for Leaders and Managers*. London: Jessica Kingsley Publishers.

Garvey, D. and Lancaster, A. (2010) *Leadership for Quality in Early Years and Playwork: Supporting Your Team to Achieve Better Outcomes for Children and Families*. London: National Children's Bureau.

Gibbs, G. (1988) *Learning by Doing: A Guide to Teaching and Learning Methods*. Oxford: Further Educational Unit, Oxford Polytechnic.

Goleman, D. (1996) *Emotional Intelligence: Why It Can Matter More Than IQ*. London: Bloomsbury.

Hardy, K., Tomlinson, J., Cruz, K. Norman, H., Whittaker, X. and Archer, N. (2022) Essential but undervalued: early years care & education during COVID-19. University of Leeds. Available at: https://childcare-during-covid.org/wp-content/uploads/2022/02/ CDC-19-Final-report.pdf.

Hopkins, B., Geangu, E. and Linkenauger, S., eds. (2017) *The Cambridge Encyclopaedia of Child Development*. Cambridge: Cambridge University Press.

Johns, C. (2000) *Becoming a Reflective Practitioner: A Reflective and Holistic Approach to Clinical Nursing, Practice Development and Clinical Supervision*. Oxford: Blackwell Science.

Keenan, T., Evans, S. and Crowley, K. (2016) *An Introduction to Child Development*. London: Sage.

Kolb, D. A. (1984) *Experiential Learning: Experience as the Source of Learning and Development.* Upper Saddle River, NJ: Prentice Hall.

Kolb, D. A. and Fry, R. (1975) Toward an applied theory of experiential learning. In: C. Cooper, ed. *Theories of Group Process.* London: John Wiley, pp. 33–56.

Luft, J. and Ingham, H. (1955) The Johari window, a graphic model of interpersonal awareness. *Proceedings of the Western Training Laboratory in Group Development.* Los Angeles, CA: University of California.

Mevawalla, Z. and Archer, N. (2022) Advocacy in early childhood education. In: S. Faircloth, ed. *Oxford Bibliographies in Education.* New York: Oxford University Press. [online] Available at: https://doi .org/10.1093/OBO/9780199756810-0291.

Moon, J. (1999) *Reflection in Learning and Professional Development.* London: Kogan Page.

Moon, J. (2004) *A Handbook on Reflective and Experiential Learning: Theory and practice.* 2nd edn. Oxon: Routledge Falmer.

Moon, J. (2005) *Learning Journals: A Handbook for Reflective Practice and Professional Development.* 2nd edn. London: Routledge.

Nagoski, E. and Nagoski, A. (2020) *Burnout: The Secret to Unlocking the Stress Cycle.* London: Vermilion/Penguin Random House.

Ortlipp, M. (2008) Keeping and using reflective journals in the qualitative research process. *The Qualitative Report*, 13(4), pp. 695–705. Available at: https://doi.org/10.46743/2160-3715/2008 .1579.

(1) Oliveira-Formosinho, J. and Formosinho, J. (2012) Towards a social science of the social: the contribution of praxeological research. *European Early Childhood Education Research Journal*, 20(4), pp. 591–606.

(2) Palaiologou, I. and Male, T. (2019) Leadership in early childhood education: the case for pedagogical praxis. *Contemporary Issues in Early Childhood*, 20(1), pp. 23–34.

(1) Pascal, C. and Bertram, T. (2012) Praxis, ethics and power: developing praxeology as a participatory paradigm for early childhood research. *European Early Childhood Education Research Journal*, 20(4), pp. 477–492. Available at: https://doi.org/10.1080/1350293X.2012.737236.

Rolfe, G., Freshwater, D. and Jasper, M. (2001) *Critical Reflection in Nursing and the Helping Professions: A User's Guide*. Basingstoke: Palgrave Macmillan.

Schön, D. A. (1983) *The Reflective Practitioner: How Professionals Think in Action*. Aldershot: Ashgate.

(2) Sims, M. (2017) Neoliberalism and early childhood. *Cogent Education*, 4(1), p. 1365411. Available at: https://doi.org/10.1080/2331186X.2017.1365411.

(3) Wilkinson, C. (2020) Imposter syndrome and the accidental academic: an autoethnographic account. *The International Journal for Academic Development*, 25(4), pp. 363–374.

(3) Wright, R. R. (2016) Comics, kitsch, and class: an autoethnographic exploration of an accidental academic. *International Journal of Qualitative Studies in Education*, 29(3), pp. 426–444.

8 Conclusion and Final Thoughts

So, here we are at the end – I hope you have found it useful. I always love the conclusion of a book and having a little time as an author to reflect on my journey.

And a journey it has certainly been! Just over two years ago, amid the global Covid-19 pandemic and in the middle of the second U.K. lockdown, I received an email asking if I'd be interested in writing a book about neuroscience. At the time, I thought that lockdown, restrictions and lots of time at home would give me plenty of time to write. And that a book on one of my favourite subjects would be finished within six months. Ha, not quite! My brain had other ideas… I found the uncertainty difficult and did not cope well with the changes the world needed to make. I didn't even have video communication software then – and now couldn't live without it. Add in other stressful situations and a (thankfully not) ovarian cancer scare – and yes, it has definitely been a journey. A journey I would not have completed without the genuine, authentic, and sincere support of Clare Ashworth, Senior Editor at Speechmark. Throughout all the trials and tribulations of the last two years Clare has been by my side, a constant, calming influence, and an absolute privilege to work with. Clare – my sincere thanks, this book is better for having been supported by your guiding hand.

Also, I would have liked this book to be a circle – well, a sphere or ball shape actually…. Oh, I know – don't say it – there's no such thing, but it would have been so helpful if there was. The reason I say this is because everything interconnects to everything else. You can't talk about environments, without adults. You can't talk about play, without behaviours… and on, and on. I hope I've made the links across the chapters – but if not, try and imagine you are reading a ball – after all we work with small children, I am sure we can imagine *anything*!

DOI: 10.4324/9781003154846-8

In terms of things that didn't quite fit. Well, I would have loved to explore polyvagal theory and the vagus nerve. We could have curiously considered praxis and praxeology (see bibliography in previous chapter). It would have been fascinating to consider the impacts of women's health within the sector, and how all of this links to neuroscience – but there's only ever so much room.

It still surprises and delights me that this is where I am now – I never intended to be a writer or a researcher. Writing books and continuing my own learning has ignited and kindled a deep love of learning and reflection. I only ever wanted to make life better for children, families and this wonderful early childhood sector I am proud to call my home. And, so I now hand this book over to you lovely reader, with my very warmest wishes. Long may we continue to uphold the dedication at the very beginning of this book – to love and support our youngest children and make a difference – every day.

> Grown-ups and children must join their forces. In order to become great, the grown-up must become humble and learn from the child.
>
> (Montessori, 1949: 417)

Reference

Montessori, M. (1949) *The Absorbent Mind*. Adyar: The Theosophical Publishing House.

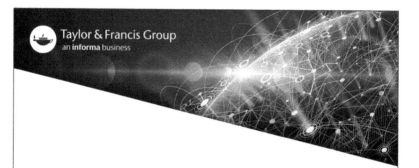